A GOD HEARS HER DEVOTIONAL

known
by
God

40 Devotions
and Insights on
Women of the Bible

Our Daily Bread
Publishing™

Known by God: 40 Devotions and Insights on Women of the Bible
© 2023 by Our Daily Bread Ministries

Devotional readings 3, 4, 11–14, 19, 23–26, 28, 29, and 32–37 were previously published over a span of years in the *Our Daily Bread* devotional booklets that are distributed around the world in more than fifty languages.

Requests for permission to quote from this book should be directed to: Permissions Department, Our Daily Bread Publishing, PO Box 3566, Grand Rapids, MI 49501, or contact us by email at permissionsdept@odb.org.

Scripture quotations, unless otherwise indicated, are taken from the Holy Bible, New Living Translation, copyright © 1996, 2004, 2015 by Tyndale House Foundation. Used by permission of Tyndale House Publishers, Inc., Carol Stream, Illinois 60188. All rights reserved.

Scripture quotations marked CSB are taken from the Christian Standard Bible®, Copyright © 2017 by Holman Bible Publishers. Used by permission. Christian Standard Bible® and CSB® are federally registered trademarks of Holman Bible Publishers.

Scripture quotations marked ESV are taken from the ESV® Bible (The Holy Bible, English Standard Version®), copyright © 2001 by Crossway, a publishing ministry of Good News Publishers. Used by permission. All rights reserved.

Scripture quotations marked NIrV are taken from the Holy Bible, New International Reader's Version®, NIrV® Copyright © 1995, 1996, 1998 by Biblica, Inc.™ Used by permission of Zondervan. All rights reserved worldwide. www.zondervan.com.

Scripture quotations marked NIV are taken from the Holy Bible, New International Version®, NIV®. Copyright © 1973, 1978, 1984, 2011 by Biblica, Inc.™ Used by permission of Zondervan. All rights reserved worldwide. www.zondervan.com.

Scripture quotations marked NKJV are taken from the New King James Version®. Copyright © 1982 by Thomas Nelson. Used by permission. All rights reserved.

Italics in Scripture reflect the author's added emphasis.

ISBN: 978-1-64070-184-7

Library of Congress Cataloging-in-Publication Data Available

Printed in China
23 24 25 26 27 28 29 30 / 8 7 6 5 4 3 2 1

Contents

PART 2: WOMEN OF THE NEW TESTAMENT

Introduction

The women writers of *Our Daily Bread* welcome you on a redemptive, life-giving journey with the women of the Bible. Whether you're familiar with these stories or reading them for the first time, you're invited to experience the nearness of the One who called each woman into a personal, transformative relationship with Him, the God attentive to every detail of her story—and yours.

During the next forty days, let God draw closer to you in your devotional time. Each devotion encourages you to walk alongside these women as they encounter the almighty, personal God—and invites you to do the same! Ponder the stories of the women of the Bible through the beautifully written devotions. Listen deeply to the Scriptures that accompany the devotional text. Voice your fears, desires, and passions to God in prayer while engaging with the prayer and meditation exercises. Finally, let the Bible—and the world of the women of the Bible—come alive, aided by historical insights, exercises with Scripture, and word studies.

For the next forty days, join us as we journey with the women of the Bible and enter into God's plans to make all things new. May you also know that God sees you. He is present in your story. And He hears your heart's cry.

You are known—and loved—by Him.

Anna Haggard
General Editor

PART 1

Women
of the
Old Testament

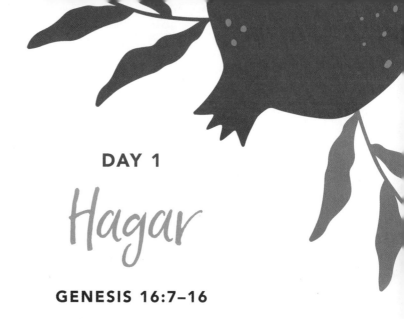

DAY 1

Hagar

GENESIS 16:7–16

The angel of the LORD found Hagar beside a spring of water in the wilderness, along the road to Shur. The angel said to her, "Hagar, Sarai's servant, where have you come from, and where are you going?"

"I'm running away from my mistress, Sarai," she replied.

The angel of the LORD to her, "Return to your mistress, and submit to her authority." Then he added, "I will give you more descendants than you can count."

And the angel also said, "You are now pregnant and will give birth to a son. You are to name him Ishmael (which means 'God hears'), for the LORD has heard your cry of distress. This son of yours will be a wild man, as untamed as a wild donkey! He will raise his fist against everyone, and everyone will be against him. Yes, he will live in open hostility against all his relatives."

Thereafter, Hagar used another name to refer to the LORD, who had spoken to her. She said, "You are the God who sees me." She also said, "Have I truly seen the One who sees me?" So that well was named Beer-lahai-roi (which means "well of the Living One who sees me"). It can still be found between Kadesh and Bered.

So Hagar gave Abram a son, and Abram named him Ishmael. Abram was eighty-six years old when Ishmael was born.

HOW GOD SEES

**She gave this name to the LORD who spoke to her:
"You are the God who sees me," for she said, "I have
now seen the One who sees me."**

GENESIS 16:13 NIV

The women from my Bible study finished their third round of good-byes as our group leader ushered them out the door. She turned to me. "Thanks for staying," she said. "I could tell something was wrong today."

I fidgeted. How could I tell a perfect wife and mother that I had another argument with my husband? I wanted to share the heartache I'd concealed behind my smile. Instead, I had a full-blown meltdown. She led me to the sofa. We cried, prayed, and shared openly. Thanking God for knowing us and loving us unconditionally, we committed to being honest as we offered one another prayer and support.

During my drive home, I thanked God for helping my friend see me.

Hagar's dysfunctional home life led her into the desert and left her physically and emotionally exposed (Genesis 16:1–6). The angel of the LORD invited her into a safe space to share honestly about her hardships and provided a promise of God's ongoing care (vv. 7–12). In an act of worship, Hagar said, "I have now seen the One who sees me" (v. 13 NIV).

When God *sees* His cherished chosen ones, He examines beyond the surface and stays for the long haul of our healing journey. He considers our deepest needs, gets up close, and stays personal. Our loving God knows us completely and reveals Himself to us intimately, as He works to fulfill all He has promised us.

—Xochitl Dixon

9

If God were to ask you, as He asked Hagar, "Where have you come from, and where are you going?" what would you tell Him?

As you begin this forty-day devotional experience, answer these two questions, sharing the highlights of your journey with God—the mountaintop experiences, smooth sailing, U-turns, roadblocks, and frustrating delays—along with whatever scenery is up ahead.

_____

_____

_____

_____

_____

_____

_____

_____

_____

_____

_____

_____

_____

_____

_____

_____

PROFILE: HAGAR

We meet Hagar on the run—escaping abuse, carrying a child—her situation desperate.

But she was not unseen.

In today's Bible reading, we read, "The angel of the LORD *found* Hagar beside a spring of water in the wilderness, along the road to Shur" (Genesis 16:7).

Many scholars believe the One Hagar met in the desert was God the Son, Jesus—who appeared to several people in the Old Testament. Before she was aware of Him, Hagar was known by God. And at one of Hagar's lowest points, God sought her out. Their encounter is remarkable: God called her by name (v. 8). He listened to her (v. 8). He entrusted great promises to her (vv. 10–12). And in turn, she became the only person in the Old Testament to name God (v. 13).

ABOUT IMAGINATIVE MEDITATION

The Bible and prayer come alive when we engage our imaginations while studying Scripture. In many of the prompts for prayer and meditation that accompany these devotions, we invite you to enter into a scene from the day's Bible reading using your mind's eye. Visualize the setting, talk with the figures in the story, and take in the sights, sounds, tastes, smells, and scenery. As you engage, don't worry about getting the right answers.

You may be thinking, *But I don't have an imagination!* If you've ever planned out your outfit the night before—choosing your top, pants, and shoes in your mind's eye—you have effectively used your imagination. If you're struggling with these exercises, imagine that you are telling the story to a child. Finally, have fun!

ENGAGE

Enter into today's Bible story by imagining that you are Hagar. Engage your five senses. As you stop by the side of the road, what does the landscape look like? What do you smell, touch, and taste? And what are your hopes and fears? Notice the Stranger at the spring. Take in His appearance. Talk to Him. Reflect on the amazing promises God gives to you. How do you respond?

_____

_____

_____

_____

_____

As you face Him, feel His love for you. What is it like to feel seen by Him? Tell Him how you feel.

_____

_____

_____

_____

_____

_____

DAY 2

Rebekah

GENESIS 24:38, 47–60

[Abraham commanded his servant], "Go instead to my **father's house**, to my relatives, and find a wife there for my son." . . .

> Hebrew *bet 'ab*; see today's biblical insight: Daily Life for a Woman of the Bible.

"Then [the servant] asked, 'Whose daughter are you?' She replied, 'I am the daughter of Bethuel, and my grandparents are Nahor and Milcah.' So I put the ring on her nose, and the bracelets on her wrists.

"Then I bowed low and worshiped the LORD. I praised the LORD, the God of my master, Abraham, because he had led me straight to my master's niece to be his son's wife. So tell me—will you or won't you show unfailing love and faithfulness to my master? Please tell me yes or no, and then I'll know what to do next."

Then Laban and Bethuel replied, "The LORD has obviously brought you here, so there is nothing we can say. Here is Rebekah; take her and go. Yes, let her be the wife of your master's son, as the LORD has directed."

When Abraham's servant heard their answer, he bowed down to the ground and worshiped the LORD. Then he brought out silver and gold jewelry and clothing and presented them to Rebekah. He also gave expensive presents to her brother and mother. Then they ate their meal, and the servant and the men with him stayed there overnight.

But early the next morning, Abraham's servant said, "Send me back to my master."

"But we want Rebekah to stay with us at least ten days," her brother and mother said. "Then she can go."

But he said, "Don't delay me. The LORD has made my mission successful; now send me back so I can return to my master."

"Well," they said, "we'll call Rebekah and ask her what she thinks." So they called Rebekah. "Are you willing to go with this man?" they asked her.

And she replied, "Yes, I will go."

So they said good-bye to Rebekah and sent her away with Abraham's servant and his men. The woman who had been Rebekah's childhood nurse went along with her. They gave her this blessing as she parted:

"Our sister, may you become
  the mother of many millions!
May your descendants be strong
  and conquer the cities of their enemies."

REBEKAH'S CHOICE

And [Rebekah] replied, "Yes, I will go."

GENESIS 24:58

After graduating from college and interviewing with three possible employers, I moved back in with my parents. One day a letter arrived announcing the job offer I'd been waiting for, but the opportunity was five hundred miles away from home. Weeks later, I decided to trust God and begin a new life.

In the ancient world, Rebekah had the chance to travel to Canaan and become Isaac's wife. Would she cling to what was familiar, or leave and try something new? The choice was hers when there was a disagreement between her family and the servant who had come to find her. Her family hesitated to let her go right away, but the servant, sent by Isaac's family, didn't want to wait.

Rebekah knew the journey could be dangerous. She'd never seen the groom-to-be and might have worried that he would be disagreeable to her or that she would be an ill-suited match for him. Still, she'd seen his family's servant thank God for leading him to her—the servant had been respectful and generous too. Most importantly, her family believed God was involved in the situation (Genesis 24:50). Rebekah chose to leave immediately (v. 58). Ultimately, her courage in facing the unknown helped confirm she was the right match for Isaac (v. 8). Her willing, bold response revealed God's wisdom in appointing Rebekah as a matriarch of God's chosen people.

Does our willingness to embrace uncertainty matter to God? Yes, because it proves we trust Him. Because He goes before us and promises to stay with us, we know He'll help us no matter what lies ahead (Deuteronomy 31:8).

—Jennifer Benson Schuldt

How does God's presence comfort you when you consider
stepping into the unknown?

_____

_____

_____

_____

_____

_____

What is the relationship between godly wisdom and facing
the future with confidence?

_____

_____

_____

_____

_____

_____

DAILY LIFE FOR A WOMAN OF THE BIBLE

She rarely had a moment to herself. From daybreak until sundown, a woman of the ancient Near East was surrounded by extended family — cousins, husband, in-laws, unmarried siblings, grandparents, or children.

The home (*bet 'ab*, literally "father's house") was the hub of the ancient world: of business, family, and the social sphere. And she was at the home's epicenter. Most women married. The matriarch was her husband's business partner—the COO (chief operating officer) to his CEO[*]—in the division of tasks among the extended family, all of whom lived together, often in the same house!

Life in the ancient Near East was uncertain, especially for a woman. While influential, she had few formal rights. And the startlingly low life expectancy for a woman in Rebekah's time—between twenty and thirty years, lower than that of a man[†]—meant that all too often a woman's life was cut short, whether from lack of access to medical care, inadequate nutrition, or complications at childbirth.

----

[*]Carol Meyers, *Rediscovering Eve: Ancient Israelite Women in Context* (Oxford: Oxford University Press, 2013), 188.
[†]Meyers, *Rediscovering Eve*, 99.

ENGAGE

Rebekah must have felt some level of uncertainty about going with Abraham's servant. Identify an area of your life that feels uncertain or unknown and talk to God about it.

_____

_____

_____

_____

_____

Dear God, help me to rely on Your faithfulness when I feel unsure about the future. Give me the courage to step forward knowing You will be with me.

Boldly ask God for what you need to take the next step in facing the future, and listen for His loving response to you.

_____

_____

_____

_____

DAY 3

Leah

GENESIS 29:16–25, 31–35

Now Laban had two daughters. The older daughter was named Leah, and the younger one was Rachel. There was no sparkle in Leah's eyes, but Rachel had a beautiful figure and a lovely face. Since Jacob was in love with Rachel, he told her father, "I'll work for you for seven years if you'll give me Rachel, your younger daughter, as my wife."

"Agreed!" Laban replied. "I'd rather give her to you than to anyone else. Stay and work with me." So Jacob worked seven years to pay for Rachel. But his love for her was so strong that it seemed to him but a few days.

Finally, the time came for him to marry her. "I have fulfilled my agreement," Jacob said to Laban. "Now give me my wife so I can sleep with her."

So Laban invited everyone in the neighborhood and prepared a wedding feast. But that night, when it was dark, Laban took Leah to Jacob, and he slept with her. (Laban had given Leah a servant, Zilpah, to be her maid.)

But when Jacob woke up in the morning—it was Leah! . . .

When the LORD saw that Leah was unloved, he enabled her to have children, but Rachel could not conceive. So Leah became pregnant and gave birth to a son. She named him **Reuben**, for she said, "The LORD has noticed my misery, and now my husband will love me."

She soon became pregnant again and gave birth to another son. She named him **Simeon**, for she said, "The LORD heard that I was unloved and has given me another son."

Then she became pregnant a third time and gave birth to another son. He was named **Levi**, for she said, "Surely this time my husband will feel affection for me, since I have given him three sons!"

Once again Leah became pregnant and gave birth to another son. She named him **Judah**, for she said, "Now I will praise the LORD!" And then she stopped having children.

Reuben means "Look, a son!" It also sounds like the Hebrew for "He has seen my misery."

Simeon probably means "one who hears."

Levi sounds like a Hebrew term that means "being attached" or "feeling affection for."

Judah is related to the Hebrew term for "praise."

SECOND BEST

[Leah] said, "Now I will praise the LORD!"

GENESIS 29:35

Leah must have laid awake all night thinking of the moment when her new husband would awaken. She knew that it was not her face he expected to see, but Rachel's. Jacob had been a victim of deception, and when he realized that a "bait and switch" had occurred, he quickly made a new deal with Laban to claim the woman he had been promised (Genesis 29:25–27).

Have you ever felt insignificant or second-best? Leah felt that way. It's seen in the names she chose for her first three sons (vv. 31–34). Reuben means "see, a son"; Simeon means "heard"; and Levi means "attached." Their names were all plays on words that indicated the lack of love she felt from Jacob. With each son's birth, she desperately hoped she would move up in Jacob's affections and earn his love. But slowly Leah's attitude changed, and she named her fourth son Judah, which means "praise" (v. 35). Though she felt unloved by her husband, perhaps she now realized she was greatly loved by God.

We can never "earn" God's love, because it's not dependent on what we do. In truth, the Bible tells us that "while we were still sinners, Christ died for us" (Romans 5:8 NIV). In God's eyes, we are worth the best that heaven could offer—the gift of His precious Son.

—Cindy Hess Kasper

When have you felt seen, known, and loved? Talk to God about it.

_____

_____

_____

_____

When have you felt unseen, unknown, or unloved?
Tell Jesus how you felt.

_____

_____

_____

_____

_____

_____

_____

_____

_____

_____

LOVE AND MARRIAGE

Weddings, at least as we know them today, didn't exist in the world of the Old Testament. That is, a couple never held a religious ceremony where they said, "I do." (*Wedding* isn't even a word in the Old Testament!) But a large celebration—filled with music, dancing, and feasting—marked the joyful occasion. In today's passage, we read of one such neighborhood gathering to celebrate Jacob's supposed marriage to Rachel (Genesis 29:22). When entering into marriage, brides like Rachel and Leah were believed to be in their teens, and grooms were more likely much older.

Did love play a role in ancient marriages? While some were in love with their spouse—as Jacob was with Rachel, leaving a devastating situation for Leah (vv. 18–20, 30)—love wasn't the primary goal: in the ancient world, the purposes of marriage were to strengthen economic interests, to forge family alliances, and, most of all, to raise children.

ENGAGE

Dialogue with Scripture in order to see it with fresh eyes. For example, who captivates your attention in today's Bible passage? Whether that person inspires you, angers you, or just makes you curious, talk to him or her about it. No topic is off-limits. Have a conversation about the events in today's story—or about something else.

_____

_____

_____

_____

_____

_____

_____

_____

_____

_____

_____

Follow-up: What did you discover about this person, God, or yourself?
Did anything come up that surprised you?

DAY 4

Rachel

GENESIS 29:31; 30:1–2, 22–24

When the LORD saw that Leah was unloved, he enabled her to have children, but Rachel **could not conceive**. . . .

> Hebrew *aqarah*; see today's word study.

When Rachel saw that she wasn't having any children for Jacob, she became jealous of her sister. She pleaded with Jacob, "Give me children, or I'll die!"

Then Jacob became furious with Rachel. "Am I God?" he asked. "He's the one who has kept you from having children!" . . .

Then God remembered Rachel's plight and answered her prayers by enabling her to have children. She became pregnant and gave birth to a son. "God has removed my disgrace," she said. And she named him Joseph, for she said, "May the LORD add yet another son to my family."

REMEMBERED IN PRAYER

Then God remembered Rachel; he listened to her.

GENESIS 30:22 NIV

In the large African church, the pastor fell to his knees, praying to God. "Remember us!" As the pastor pleaded, the crowd responded, crying, "Remember us, Lord!" Watching this moment on YouTube, I was surprised that I shed tears too. The prayer was recorded months earlier. Yet it recalled childhood times when I heard our family's pastor make the same plea to God. "Remember us, Lord!"

Hearing that prayer as a child, I'd wrongly assumed that God sometimes forgets about us. But God is all-knowing (Psalm 147:5; 1 John 3:20), He always see us (Psalm 33:13–15), and He loves us beyond measure (Ephesians 3:17–19).

Even more, as we see in the Hebrew word *zakar*, meaning "remember," when God remembers us, He acts for us. *Zakar* also means "to act on a person's behalf." Thus, when God "remembered" Noah and "all the wild animals and livestock with him in the boat," He then "sent a wind to blow across the earth, and the floodwaters began to recede" (Genesis 8:1). When God "remembered" barren Rachel, He "answered her prayers by enabling her to have children. She became pregnant and gave birth to a son" (30:22–23).

What a great plea of trust to ask God in prayer to remember us! He'll decide how He answers, but we can pray knowing that our humble request asks God to move.

—Patricia Raybon

27

In what area of your life do you need God to remember you?

_____

_____

_____

_____

_____

_____

Talk to Him about it. How does God respond to you?

_____

_____

_____

_____

_____

_____

Word Study

CHILDLESS [NLT translation—*could not conceive*]

aqarah (Genesis 29:31)

In the ancient Near East, being a mother—having children—was the primary purpose of a woman's life. Infertility (*aqarah*, being "childless, barren, sterile") was devastating, seen as shameful, even viewed as a divine curse. Amazingly, almost all the matriarchs—including Rachel, Sarah, and Rebekah—experienced infertility. In fact, the suffering experienced as a result of infertility is a common thread knitting together the lives of women of faith throughout the Bible (see Hannah, 1 Samuel 1:2; the wife of Manoah, Judges 13:2–3; the Shunammite woman, 2 Kings 4:14–15; Elizabeth, Luke 1:7).

Their common experience of barrenness, along with God's intervention in enabling them to conceive, brings front and center the problem that was all too visible to the women of the Bible: we have limited control over our lives. The men and women of the Bible recognized, and verbalized, that it was only through God's intervention that a childless family could conceive (Genesis 16:2; 30:2).

ENGAGE

Whether you're in a season of waiting or abundant provision, take a couple of minutes to draw near to God and express your trust in Him. Adapt one of the Scripture passages on the next page into your own prayer to God.

_____

_____

_____

_____

_____

_____

_____

_____

_____

_____

_____

_____

God is our refuge and strength,
A very present help in trouble. . . .

Be still, and know that I am God;
I will be exalted among the nations,
I will be exalted in the earth!
The LORD of hosts is with us;
The God of Jacob is our refuge. (Psalm 46:1, 10–11 NKJV)

> My heart, O God, is steadfast,
> my heart is steadfast;
> I will sing and make music. . . .
>
> I will praise you, Lord, among the nations;
> I will sing of you among the peoples.
> For great is your love, reaching to the heavens;
> your faithfulness reaches to the skies. (Psalm 57:7, 9–10 NIV)

I remain confident of this:
I will see the goodness of the LORD
in the land of the living.
Wait for the LORD;
be strong and take heart.
and wait for the LORD. (Psalm 27:13–14 NIV)

DAY 5

Tamar

GENESIS 38:6–10, 13–19, 24–30

In the course of time, Judah arranged for his firstborn son, Er, to marry a young woman named Tamar. But Er was a wicked man in the LORD's sight, so the LORD took his life. Then Judah said to Er's brother Onan, **"Go and marry Tamar, as our law requires of the brother of a man who has died. You must produce an heir for your brother."**

> This refers to an ancient marriage practice; see today's biblical insight: Levirate Marriage.

But Onan was not willing to have a child who would not be his own heir. So whenever he had intercourse with his brother's wife, he spilled the semen on the ground. This prevented her from having a child who would belong to his brother. But the LORD considered it evil for Onan to deny a child to his dead brother. So the LORD took Onan's life, too. . . .

Someone told Tamar, "Look, your father-in-law is going up to Timnah to shear his sheep."

Tamar was aware that Shelah had grown up, but no arrangements had been made for her to come and marry him. So she changed out of her widow's clothing and covered herself with a veil to disguise herself. Then she sat beside the road at the entrance to the village of Enaim, which is on the road to Timnah. Judah noticed her and thought she was a prostitute, since she had covered her face. So he stopped and propositioned her. "Let me have sex with you," he said, not realizing that she was his own daughter-in-law.

"How much will you pay to have sex with me?" Tamar asked.

"I'll send you a young goat from my flock," Judah promised.

"But what will you give me to guarantee that you will send the goat?" she asked.

"What kind of guarantee do you want?" he replied.

She answered, "Leave me your identification seal and its cord and the walking stick you are carrying." So Judah gave them to her. Then he had intercourse with her, and she became pregnant. Afterward she went back home, took off her veil, and put on her widow's clothing as usual. . . .

About three months later, Judah was told, "Tamar, your daughter-in-law, has acted like a prostitute. And now, because of this, she's pregnant."

"Bring her out, and let her be burned!" Judah demanded.

But as they were taking her out to kill her, she sent this message to her father-in-law: "The man who owns these things made me pregnant. Look closely. Whose seal and cord and walking stick are these?"

Judah recognized them immediately and said, "She is more righteous than I am, because I didn't arrange for her to marry my son Shelah." And Judah never slept with Tamar again.

When the time came for Tamar to give birth, it was discovered that she was carrying twins. While she was in labor, one of the babies reached out his hand. The midwife grabbed it and tied a scarlet string around the child's wrist, announcing, "This one came out first." But then he pulled back his hand, and out came his brother! "What!" the midwife exclaimed. "How did you break out first?" So he was named Perez. Then the baby with the scarlet string on his wrist was born, and he was named Zerah.

THE DIAMOND IN YOU

**He who began a good work in you will carry it on to
completion until the day of Christ Jesus.**

PHILIPPIANS 1:6 NIV

A raw diamond needs a trained eye to spot its potential. We might look at a kimberlite rock and judge it worthless because it looks rough and fragmented, not realizing that the rock contains diamonds waiting to be cut and polished.

At first glance Tamar's life didn't seem like it could produce a diamond. After marrying a man whose actions were deemed by God as evil and worthy of death, she married his brother. But his refusal to have a child with her to fulfill the levirate marriage requirement (Deuteronomy 25:5; see today's insight) caused God to put him to death too. In desperation, Tamar concocted a plan to gain a child through her father-in-law—Judah, son of Jacob—by pretending to be a prostitute after Judah reneged on the promise to give her his third son in marriage.

Tamar's story sounds like a tawdry tabloid story—the kind we want to turn away from because it seems too messy. No matter how dysfunctional the situation, God chose not to turn away. He chipped away at the rock of this family line from generation to generation until eventually a flawless diamond was produced: Jesus. The Savior who by one touch made the unclean clean.

What God did through Tamar's family line He can do in one person's life. He takes even the messiest situations and "works for the good of those who love him" (Romans 8:28 NIV). You can trust that as He works in your life, chipping away the areas that mar the diamond in you, He has your good in mind.

—Linda Washington

34

What do you sense God working on in your life?

_____

_____

_____

_____

_____

_____

What has someone affirmed in you that was hidden or unknown to you?
What difference has that made in your life?

_____

_____

_____

_____

_____

_____

_____

_____

LEVIRATE MARRIAGE

The practice of levirate marriage, instructed in Deuteronomy 25:5–10, calls for the brother of a man who dies without heirs to marry the deceased brother's widow. A child born from that union would be considered the deceased brother's child and heir—"so that his name will not be forgotten" (v. 6).

While levirate marriage's stated intent is for the deceased's line to continue (v. 6), one effect of levirate marriage was preserving social standing and economic protection for widows. A woman in the ancient Near East would be given in marriage with a dowry from her father's household—transferring her place in society and the responsibility for her economic protection to her father-in-law's household. Levirate marriage gave a widowed woman a way to retain her standing in her father-in-law's household and have children who could later provide for her. So when Judah instructed his widowed daughter-in-law Tamar to go back to her parents' home—with no intention of allowing her to marry his remaining son (Genesis 38:11)—he stripped her of economic security and standing in society. Tamar's drastic ploy (vv. 14–19) led Judah to repent of the great injustice he'd done to her (v. 26).

ENGAGE

Identify an area of your life where God has been chipping away at your rough edges to reveal the diamond in you. How have you experienced this process of transformation? Has it been disorienting? Exciting? Painful? Journal to God about your experience of the changes, being honest with Him about your fears and hopes as you're being shaped and polished.

Shiphrah and Puah

EXODUS 1:11–21

So the Egyptians made the Israelites their slaves. They appointed brutal slave drivers over them, hoping to wear them down with crushing labor. They forced them to build the cities of Pithom and Rameses as supply centers for the king. But the more the Egyptians oppressed them, the more the Israelites multiplied and spread, and the more alarmed the Egyptians became. So the Egyptians worked the people of Israel without mercy. They made their lives bitter, forcing them to mix mortar and make bricks and do all the work in the fields. They were ruthless in all their demands.

Then Pharaoh, the king of Egypt, gave this order to the Hebrew midwives, Shiphrah and Puah: "When you help the Hebrew women as they give birth, **watch as they deliver**. If the baby is a boy, kill him; if it is a girl, let her live." But because the midwives feared God, they refused to obey the king's orders. They allowed the boys to live, too.

> Literal Hebrew translation: *look upon the two stones*; perhaps the reference is to a birthstool—see today's word study.

So the king of Egypt called for the midwives. "Why have you done this?" he demanded. "Why have you allowed the boys to live?"

"The Hebrew women are not like the Egyptian women," the midwives replied. "They are more vigorous and have their babies so quickly that we cannot get there in time."

So God was good to the midwives, and the Israelites continued to multiply, growing more and more powerful. And because the midwives feared God, he gave them families of their own.

DOING WHAT'S RIGHT

Because the midwives feared God, they refused to obey the king's orders. They allowed the boys to live.

EXODUS 1:17

When Germany invaded the Netherlands during World War II, Corrie ten Boom was a middle-aged woman happily working in her father's watch repair shop. Despite the danger, Corrie and her family became active in the resistance and hid Jews in their home. Corrie later stated, "When a train goes through a tunnel and it gets dark, you don't throw away the ticket and jump off. You sit still and trust the engineer." She held on to her faith in God and kept doing what was right.

In Exodus, we see another story of faith and courage. When a wicked king came into power in Egypt, he mistrusted the Israelites living in his land and began treating them harshly (Exodus 1:8–11). "But the more they were oppressed, the more they multiplied" (v. 12 NIV). And so he ordered the Hebrew midwives, Shiphrah and Puah, to kill any baby boys they helped deliver. "The midwives, however, feared God" and performed their work with loving care just as before (v. 17 NIV).

When the Hebrew boys continued to be born and thrive, the king (one of the most powerful rulers of the world) once again summoned the midwives. But the women did not back down. As a result of their faith in God and obedience to Him, "[God] gave them families of their own" (v. 21 NIV).

You too may be in a situation where you know what's right but fear the consequences of doing it. Take courage and trust God to help you through.

—Alyson Kieda

Identify a situation or circumstance where God may be
calling you to boldly rise up.

_____

_____

_____

_____

_____

_____

Ask God for what you need to face the situation with faith and courage,
listening for His loving response to you.

_____

_____

_____

_____

_____

_____

Word Study

BIRTHSTOOL

'obnayim (Exodus 1:16)

In the ancient Near East, a woman would squat on a birthstool (the Hebrew word *'obnayim*) during childbirth. In Exodus 1, the pharaoh of Egypt—when commanding the Hebrew midwives to commit infanticide—made mention of this delivery stool: "When you serve as midwife to the Hebrew women and see them on the birthstool [*'obnayim*], if it is a son, you shall kill him" (v. 16 ESV).

The birthstool was likely made of two parts. In fact, one of the ways *birthstool* has been more literally translated is "two stones." (In verse 16, the more exact translation of Pharaoh's words may be "look upon the two stones.") In literature from the ancient Near East, women are recorded as crouching on two bricks during labor. And, fascinatingly, the only other Bible reference to the word *'obnayim* is of a potter's wheel (Jeremiah 18:3), also made of two parts.

In today's Bible passage, the midwives defied the pharaoh's orders by saying that the Hebrew women, being "vigorous," delivered the babies before the midwives arrived (Exodus 1:19). Because they protected innocent life, God blessed these courageous women.

ENGAGE

Identify a situation that you cannot face on your own. In your imagination, visualize the scene—the who, what, when, and where—placing yourself in the physical space. Now, imagine Jesus, your loving Savior, is physically present in the space with you. What is it like having Jesus with you, in your situation? Is Jesus looking at you? Is He placing a reassuring hand on your shoulder? And what does He want you to know amid your struggle? Tell Jesus how you feel.

When you cannot face a situation on your own, remember: God is with you.

DAY 7

Jochebed

EXODUS 2:1–10; HEBREWS 11:23

About this time, a **man and woman** from the tribe of Levi got married. The woman became pregnant and gave birth to a son. She **saw that he was a special baby** and kept him hidden for three months. But when she could no longer hide him, she got a basket made of papyrus reeds and waterproofed it with tar and pitch. She put the baby in the basket and laid it among the reeds along the bank of the Nile River. The baby's sister then stood at a distance, watching to see what would happen to him.

Exodus 6:20 identifies this couple as Amram and Jochebed.

"Longing to keep him" is a closer Hebrew translation, according to Douglas K. Stuart, *The American Commentary: Exodus* (Logos Bible Software, 2006).

Soon Pharaoh's daughter came down to bathe in the river, and her attendants walked along the riverbank. When the princess saw the basket among the reeds, she sent her maid to get it for her. When the princess opened it, she saw the baby. The little boy was crying, and she felt sorry for him. "This must be one of the Hebrew children," she said.

Then the baby's sister approached the princess. "Should I go and find one of the Hebrew women to nurse the baby for you?" she asked.

"Yes, do!" the princess replied. So the girl went and called the baby's mother.

"Take this baby and nurse him for me," the princess told the baby's mother. "I will pay you for your help." So the woman took her baby home and nursed him.

Later, when the boy was older, his mother brought him back to Pharaoh's daughter, who adopted him as her own son. The princess named him Moses, for she explained, "I lifted him out of the water."

It was by faith that Moses' parents hid him for three months when he was born. They saw that God had given them an unusual child, and they were not afraid to disobey the king's command.

FEARLESS

It was by faith that Moses' parents hid him . . . [because] they were not afraid to disobey the king's command.

HEBREWS 11:23

The joy of another long-awaited pregnancy likely turned to despair when she heard the latest devastating decree issued by the Egyptian pharaoh: all Hebrew baby boys were to be killed to keep the Israelites from becoming too numerous. Jochebed's heart must have been gripped with fear as she wrestled through what she would do if the baby in her womb was a boy.

After giving birth to a little boy, Jochebed longed to keep this baby she already loved (see Scripture text note), so she devised a risky plan that required choosing fearless faith in perilous circumstances. With the help of her family, Jochebed did everything in her power to protect the life of her child. Jochebed hid Moses for three months in her home and then concealed him in a basket in the river. Although Moses was discovered by Pharaoh's daughter, by God's gracious provision Jochebed was summoned and asked to nurse the baby. She courageously raised Moses until he was old enough to live in the palace, protected by Pharaoh's daughter.

Jochebed did all this because she was "not afraid" of Pharaoh's orders (Hebrews 11:23). She was fearless in choosing obedience to God.

We can follow in the spirit of fearless Jochebed. To be fearless might mean befriending a refugee family even though friends express concern. Or serving in a ministry to the marginalized when others shy away. Or speaking of faith when tempted to stay quiet. Fearless not because we control the outcome, but fearless "by faith" (v. 23): entrusting ourselves and our situations to God's loving care.

—Lisa M. Samra

46

Has your love or affection for someone ever moved you to act courageously on their behalf, as Jochebed's did? Write about it.

_____

_____

_____

_____

_____

In a situation where you want to be fearless, identify barriers that could be preventing you from rising up to accept that invitation. Without judging yourself, talk to God about the barrier(s). What's Jesus's loving response to you?

_____

_____

_____

_____

_____

_____

_____

_____

ABOUT THE PENTATEUCH

The first five books of the Bible (Genesis through Deuteronomy) are called the *Pentateuch*, which simply means "five books." What's the Pentateuch about? A central theme is humanity's struggle to live in God's presence in the land as He intended. The first human couple live in harmony with God only briefly before their disobedience results in their exile from the garden (Genesis 3:23–24).

But God doesn't give up on humanity. Beginning with a second couple—Abraham and Sarah—God works to show humanity the way back into His presence. God calls Abraham to a land, where, God promises, Abraham's descendants would bless all people (12:1–4). But although Abraham obeys God and arrives in that promised land, Canaan, he never experiences it fully as his home, living instead as a "stranger" there (23:3–4).

In Exodus, we find that God had kept His promise to Abraham of many descendants (1:7), but His people were being oppressed in Egypt (vv. 13–14), far from the promised land. So God works through courageous women to save the life of Moses (1:16–19; 2:1–9), who would become the most significant figure in the Pentateuch (Deuteronomy 34:9–10). Through Moses, God delivered His people from Egypt, drew His people to Himself (Exodus 19:4; 3:12), and revealed to Israel how to live in His presence. At the close of the Pentateuch, God's people wait just outside the promised land.

ENGAGE

Read Exodus 2:1–10 and Hebrews 11:23 a second time. What part of Jochebed's story seems to be speaking directly to your heart? Stop. Give yourself space to reflect on that part of the story along with God. If you're feeling stuck, ask Him, What are Your invitations to me through this story?

DAY 8

Miriam

EXODUS 15:19–21

When Pharaoh's horses, chariots, and charioteers rushed into the sea, the LORD brought the water crashing down on them. But the people of Israel had walked through the middle of the sea on dry ground!

Then Miriam the **prophet**, Aaron's sister, took a tambourine and led all the women as they played their tambourines and danced. And Miriam sang this song:

Hebrew *nebiah*; see today's biblical insight: Women Prophets in the Bible.

> "Sing to the LORD,
>   for he has triumphed gloriously;
> he has hurled both horse and rider
>   into the sea."

REJOICING IN VICTORY

Sing to the LORD, for he is highly exalted.

EXODUS 15:21 NIV

Like Miriam in the Old Testament, I grew up as the only girl among brothers. Also like Miriam, my ancestors were slaves. Unlike Miriam, my parents were not. But as children of poor sharecroppers, my parents experienced inequality in Jim Crow South. But they trusted God's love and faithfulness despite that situation. They left the South like many African Americans between 1916 and 1970, praying for better opportunities for jobs and schools in the North. When my brothers and I graduated from college, they thanked God for helping us to achieve what our ancestors could only dream about.

When she looked at her baby brother Moses, Miriam probably didn't have a clue of what God would eventually do to free their people from slavery. Yet before God used Moses to deliver their people, He first used her to deliver her brother from the pharaoh's death edict by watching over the basket that carried him to safety. Though she had to wait several decades for deliverance, she watched as God kept the promise later made to Moses to free their people. As a leader (Micah 6:4), prophet (Exodus 15:20), and worshipper, Miriam led the women in celebrating God's spectacular deliverance of His people out of slavery through the Red Sea.

Miriam's and my parents' celebrations of victory started with the knowledge of God's love and faithfulness. As we meditate on what we know about God, every day can be a victory celebration, even if nothing seems to change about our lives. Let's join in Miriam's song, "Sing to the LORD, for he is highly exalted" (Exodus 15:21 NIV).

—Linda Washington

51

What about God's character (for example, His nearness, tenderness, power, greatness) have you found especially meaningful in your current season?

_____

_____

_____

_____

_____

_____

_____

ENGAGE

As Miriam did in her song (Exodus 15:21), celebrate a time God helped you, rescued you, or walked with you during a challenging season.

_____

_____

_____

_____

_____

WOMEN PROPHETS IN THE BIBLE

Miriam is the first woman in the Hebrew Scriptures to be identified as a prophet (Exodus 15:20). The others include Deborah (Judges 4:4), Huldah (2 Kings 22:14; 2 Chronicles 34:22), and Noadiah, whom Nehemiah identifies as a false prophet who discouraged his work (Nehemiah 6:14).

What did it mean to be a prophet? The Hebrew word for prophet (*nabi*, or *nebiah* if feminine) is from the verb *naba*, which means "to call." This gets at the heart of what a prophet was—someone called to speak for God, to whom God would reveal what to say. Prophets were those trusted to speak for God, and would often be consulted by those who wanted to know God's will. But true prophets would also speak as directed by God, even when it was unpopular and unwanted.

In the ancient Near East, it does not appear to have been particularly uncommon or surprising for there to be female prophets. In a patriarchal culture, it would have been difficult for women to access many other positions of power. But both male and female prophets found their roles outside of the typical social power hierarchy: a true prophet was gifted and called solely by God.

DAY 9

Rahab

JOSHUA 2:1–9, 11

The two [Israelite spies] set out and came to the house of a prostitute named Rahab and stayed there that night.

But someone told the king of Jericho, "Some Israelites have come here tonight to spy out the land." So the king of Jericho sent orders to Rahab: "Bring out the men who have come into your house, for they have come here to spy out the whole land."

Rahab had hidden the two men, but she replied, "Yes, the men were here earlier, but I didn't know where they were from. They left the town at dusk, as the gates were about to close. I don't know where they went. If you hurry, you can probably catch up with them." (Actually, she had taken them up to the roof and hidden them beneath bundles of flax she had laid out.) So the king's men went looking for the spies along the road leading to the shallow crossings of the Jordan River. And as soon as the king's men had left, the gate of Jericho was shut.

Before the spies went to sleep that night, Rahab went up on the roof to talk with them. "I know the LORD has given you this land," she told them. "We are all afraid of you. Everyone in the land is living in terror. . . . For the LORD your God is the supreme God of the heavens above and the earth below.

DEFIANCE FOR DELIVERANCE

**She had taken them up to the roof and hidden them
beneath bundles of flax she had laid out.**

JOSHUA 2:6

When she refused to give up her bus seat to a white man, Rosa Parks had to draw on her faith for the courage to disobey the unjust segregation laws of her day. Rosa credited God for giving her "the strength to endure whatever [she] had to face."*

Her defiance triggered a wave of protests that ultimately changed the course of American history. She was later awarded the Congressional Gold Medal in recognition of her role in the civil rights movement.

Millenia earlier, another woman drew on her new belief in God to make a courageous stand on behalf of His people. During their reconnaissance mission to Jericho, the Israelite spies stayed at Rahab's house. When the king sent men to search out the spies, Rahab hid them "under the stalks of flax she had laid out on the roof" (Joshua 2:6 NIV). Harboring them would likely have cost her life had they been found.

In protecting the spies, Rahab defied the king and aligned herself with what she knew to be true about God and His purposes. God recognized her courageous faith (Hebrews 11:31), spared her entire household, and wove her story into the lineage of Jesus (Matthew 1:1, 5).

Aligning ourselves with God's purposes may not put our lives at risk, as it did for Rosa and Rahab. Yet it will require courageous defiance to stand firmly in faith when the world around us thinks differently.

—Kirsten Holmberg

---

*David Briggs, "Faith Guided Rosa Parks' Actions," *Chicago Tribune*, January 20, 1995, https://www.chicagotribune.com/news/ct-xpm-1995-01-20-9501200112-story.html.

Do you see yourself as defiant? If so, what are you usually defiant about? Is it a defiance aligned with God's purposes?

_____

_____

_____

_____

_____

What is one way you're being drawn to align with God's ways now? Talk to God about it. How does He respond to you?

_____

_____

_____

_____

_____

_____

WOMEN IN JESUS'S FAMILY TREE

Rahab and four other women—Tamar, Ruth, Bathsheba, and Mary—are included in Christ's genealogy found in the gospel of Matthew (1:3–6, 17). Why did the author feature these five particular women?

Having the right reputation and family upbringing—being Jewish—was significant to Matthew's audience. Yet except for Mary, each woman identified in Jesus's family tree is *gentile*: Tamar and Rahab are Canaanites. Ruth is a Moabite. And Bathsheba had once married into a gentile family ("wife of Uriah the Hittite," 2 Samuel 11:3), making her gentile by association. As gentiles, they were outsiders.

In his selection of these five women, Matthew seems to say, Pay attention! This is what God's new kingdom is going to be like: wide open to outsiders, to the marginalized, and to those with controversial pasts (see the scandalous pregnancies of Mary, Tamar, and Bathsheba in Luke 1:26–48; Genesis 38:13–18; 2 Samuel 11:2–4!). In his genealogy, Matthew previews the radical message of the gospel that—no matter her reputation, family history, or social status—through faith everyone could be welcomed into God's family.

ENGAGE

In this exercise, enter into today's Bible story by imagining that you are Rahab. Use your five senses. In a few minutes the king's messengers will be at your door, so why are you willing to take such a risk on behalf of foreigners—enemies no less? Are you feeling trapped? Reckless? Courageous? What is it that you want? Are you terrified of the spies' God? Drawn to Him? Both?

_____

_____

_____

_____

_____

When the king's messenger shows up at your door asking you to betray these two men, what is your response?

_____

_____

_____

_____

Aligning ourselves with God's purposes may not put our lives at risk, but it will require defiance to stand firmly in faith when the world around us thinks differently.

DAY 10

Deborah

JUDGES 4:4–10, 14–16; 5:1–3

Deborah, the **wife of Lappidoth**, was a prophet who was judging Israel at that time. She would sit under the Palm of Deborah, between Ramah and Bethel in the hill country of Ephraim, and the Israelites would go to her for judgment. One day she sent for Barak son of Abinoam, who lived in Kedesh in the land of Naphtali. She said to him, "This is what the LORD, the God of Israel, commands you: Call out 10,000 warriors from the tribes of Naphtali and Zebulun at Mount Tabor. And I will call out Sisera, commander of Jabin's army, along with his chariots and warriors, to the Kishon River. There I will give you victory over him."

Hebrew *'eset lapidot*; the words can also be translated "woman of torches" or "fiery woman"; see today's biblical insight— Profile: Deborah.

Barak told her, "I will go, but only if you go with me."

"Very well," she replied, "I will go with you. But you will receive no honor in this venture, for the LORD's victory over Sisera will be at the hands of a woman." So Deborah went with Barak to Kedesh. At Kedesh, Barak called together the tribes of Zebulun and Naphtali, and 10,000 warriors went up with him. Deborah also went with him. . . .

Then Deborah said to Barak, "Get ready! This is the day the LORD will give you victory over Sisera, for the LORD is marching ahead of you." So Barak led his 10,000 warriors down the slopes of Mount Tabor into battle. When Barak attacked, the LORD threw Sisera and all his chariots and warriors into a panic. Sisera leaped down from his chariot and escaped on foot. Then Barak chased the chariots and the enemy army all the way to Harosheth-haggoyim, killing all of Sisera's warriors. Not a single one was left alive. . . .

On that day Deborah and Barak son of Abinoam sang this song:

"Israel's leaders took charge,
   and the people gladly followed.
Praise the LORD!

"Listen, you kings!
   Pay attention, you mighty rulers!
For I will sing to the LORD.
   I will make music to the LORD, the God of Israel."

RETURN THE PRAISES

On that day Deborah and Barak son of Abinoam sang this song: . . . "I will make music to the LORD, the God of Israel."

JUDGES 5:1, 3

Nice job. Way to go. Who doesn't love a sincere compliment? I sure do. But I noticed one of my friends always returned a compliment with the words, "To God be the glory." "You knocked that out of the park," I'd overhear someone praise her performance. "To God be the glory" would be her response.

I used to chuckle because it was so predictable. But then I read Deborah's song, her words of celebration after the defeat of Israel's enemy Sisera, who was the commander of the army of Canaan (Judges 4:1–7). In the triumphant song (Judges 5), Deborah basically says, "To God be the glory."

This powerful woman of God had guided the possibly scared Barak into battle. Even though she had told him God was sending him to conquer Sisera, Barak insisted that Deborah join him. Not one to back down or to mince words, this woman was sure to let Barak know that if she accompanied him, he would not get the honor of taking out his enemy.

But when Deborah proclaims God's faithfulness in the victorious battle, she doesn't dare say "I told you so." Her praises are to God. Deborah recognizes who has truly delivered the enemy on this day. "I will praise the LORD, the God of Israel, in song," she proclaims (5:3 NIV).

I want to be more like Deborah and return each compliment with praise to the One who really did the work. God is the one who deserves the glory.

—Katara Patton

PROFILE: DEBORAH

Set between Israel's conquest of Canaan and the monarchy's establishment, the book of Judges describes a chaotic period during which judges emerged and ruled in Israel. Some judges appear to have been esteemed leaders during times of relative calm (Judges 10:1–5; 12:7–15). Others emerge in response to military conflict or crisis before judging Israel (for example, Jephthah, 12:1–7). Some leaders identified as "rescuers" are not explicitly called *judges* (3:9–11, 15).

In this context, we are told of the remarkable Deborah, the only leader in Judges identified as both a prophet and a judge (4:4). As a judge, Deborah played a daily role administering justice (v. 5). As a prophet, she also communicated God's military orders to the commander Barak.

Judges describes Deborah as *'eset lapidot*, a Hebrew phrase usually translated "wife of Lappidoth" (v. 4). But *lapidot* can also be translated "torches." Translating the phrase as "woman of torches," or "fiery woman," offers a compelling portrait of Deborah's role in Judges. Like a torch, she ignites the military commander Barak (whose name means "lightning") into action (vv. 6–10, 14). In Deborah and Barak's victory song, Deborah is described as a "mother for Israel" (5:7), through whom God brought peace (v. 31).

"*This is the day the* LORD *will give you victory . . . for the* LORD *is marching ahead of you.*"

JUDGES 4:14

ENGAGE

What current situation in your life causes you to say, "To God be the glory"? Tell Him.

DAY 11

Naomi

RUTH 1:15–22

"Look," Naomi said to her, "your sister-in-law has gone back to her people and to her gods. You should do the same."

But Ruth replied, "Don't ask me to leave you and turn back. Wherever you go, I will go; wherever you live, I will live. Your people will be my people, and your God will be my God. Wherever you die, I will die, and there I will be buried. May the LORD punish me severely if I allow anything but death to separate us!" When Naomi saw that Ruth was determined to go with her, she said nothing more.

So the two of them continued on their journey. When they came to Bethlehem, the entire town was excited by their arrival. "Is it really Naomi?" the women asked.

"Don't call me **Naomi**," she responded. "Instead, call me **Mara**, for the Almighty has made life very bitter for me. I went away full, but the LORD has brought me home *Naomi* means "pleasant"; *Mara* means "bitter." empty. Why call me Naomi when the LORD has caused me to suffer and the Almighty has sent such tragedy upon me?"

So Naomi returned from Moab, accompanied by her daughter-in-law Ruth, the young Moabite woman. They arrived in Bethlehem in late spring, at the beginning of the barley harvest.

NAMED BY GOD

"Don't call me Naomi," she responded. "Instead, call me Mara, for the Almighty has made life very bitter for me."

RUTH 1:20

Riptide. Batgirl. Jumpstart. These are a few names given to counselors at the summer camp our family attends every year. Created by their peers, the camp nicknames usually derive from an embarrassing incident, a funny habit, or a favorite hobby.

Nicknames aren't limited to camp—we even find them used in the Bible. For example, Jesus dubs the apostles James and John the "Sons of Thunder" (Mark 3:17). It is rare in Scripture for someone to give themselves a nickname, yet it happens when a woman named Naomi asks people to call her Mara, which means "bitterness," because both her husband and two sons had died. She felt that God had made her life bitter (Ruth 1:20).

The new name Naomi gave herself didn't stick, however, because those devastating losses were not the end of her story. In the midst of her sorrow, God had blessed her with a loving daughter-in-law, Ruth, who eventually remarried and had a son, creating a family for Naomi again.

Although we might sometimes be tempted to give ourselves bitter nicknames, like "failure" or "unloved," based on difficulties we've experienced or mistakes we've made, those names are not the end of our stories. We can replace those labels with the name God has given each of us, "loved one" (Romans 9:25 NIV), and look for the ways He's providing for us in even the most challenging of times.

—Lisa M. Samra

What labels have others given to you? What labels have you taken on yourself? Talk to God about them. What does Jesus want you to know about these labels versus the way He sees you?

_____

_____

_____

_____

_____

Look at a list of how God sees His beloved children:

Loved (Romans 9:25)

Chosen (Ephesians 1:4–5)

Forgiven (Ephesians 1:7)

Honored (Psalm 91:14–16)

Powerful in Christ (Romans 8:11)

Called (Romans 8:28)

Friend of God (John 15:15)

God's masterpiece (Ephesians 2:10)

Redeemed (Ephesians 1:7)

New (2 Corinthians 5:17)

Which name or truth might God be inviting you to believe on a whole new level? Talk with Jesus about it.

_____

_____

_____

_____

WIDOWS IN ANCIENT ISRAEL

Naomi is one of the heroines of the book of Ruth. Her leading role, in its time and context, is rather extraordinary: as a widow, she would've been perceived as a minor character in ancient Israel. Why? Outside the family structure, widows were often oppressed, impoverished, and ignored. In fact, in Scripture, widows are classified as a vulnerable group, along with orphans and immigrants (Exodus 22:22; Deuteronomy 14:29; 24:19; Isaiah 1:17).

God called the Israelites to care for these marginalized groups. But the Israelites often fell short, sometimes even exploiting the very people God had entrusted to their protection and care. In times of injustice, God became their personal champion: "I will protect the orphans who remain among you. Your widows, too, can depend on me for help" (Jeremiah 49:11; also see Deuteronomy 10:18). We see God take up Naomi's cause in the book of Ruth: behind the scenes, and through the faithfulness of Ruth and Boaz, God redeems Naomi's situation, placing her in a family, restoring her financially, and providing her an heir (through Ruth and Boaz's union) who is in the line of Christ.

ENGAGE

Engage with today's Bible reading in the same way you'd savor a flavorful, warm, and nourishing meal. Go back and read Ruth 1:15–22 again, slowly tasting its richness and taking time to enjoy its depth of meaning. Choose one morsel of the passage—a word, phrase, or sentence—and spend some quiet time with this Scripture.

Whatever morsel of Scripture you are drawn to, ask God, What is Your invitation for me through the text?

ABOUT A DEVOTIONAL READING OF SCRIPTURE

Today is a great example of how you can engage in a slow, interactive reading of Scripture. Amid chaotic schedules, prayerfully reading the Bible one "morsel" at a time provides a space for savoring and taking joy in the Bible.

While prayerfully reading Scripture, you select one short, focused Bible passage, letting it soak deeply into your mind and heart. Listen to God's heart through the text, inviting the Holy Spirit to share the truths God may have for you through the passage. This is not performance-based, so don't worry if nothing jumps out at you during your reading; instead see the time as an opportunity to have a two-way conversation with God—to grow in intimacy with Him—while reading the Bible.

71

DAY 12

Ruth

RUTH 2:1–12, 19–20

Now there was a wealthy and influential man in Bethlehem named Boaz, who was a relative of Naomi's husband, Elimelech.

One day Ruth the Moabite said to Naomi, "Let me go out into the harvest fields to pick up the stalks of grain left behind by anyone who is kind enough to let me do it."

Naomi replied, "All right, my daughter, go ahead." So Ruth went out to gather grain behind the harvesters. And as it happened, she found herself working in a field that belonged to Boaz, the relative of her father-in-law, Elimelech.

While she was there, Boaz arrived from Bethlehem and greeted the harvesters. "The LORD be with you!" he said.

"The LORD bless you!" the harvesters replied.

Then Boaz asked his foreman, "Who is that young woman over there? Who does she belong to?"

And the foreman replied, "She is the young woman from Moab who came back with Naomi. She asked me this morning if she could gather grain behind the harvesters. She has been hard at work ever since, except for a few minutes' rest in the shelter."

Boaz went over and said to Ruth, "Listen, my daughter. Stay right here with us when you gather grain; don't go to any other fields. Stay right behind the young women working in my field. See which part of the field they are harvesting, and then follow them. I have warned the young men not to treat you roughly. And when you are thirsty, help yourself to the water they have drawn from the well."

Ruth fell at his feet and thanked him warmly. "What have I done to deserve such kindness?" she asked. "I am only a foreigner."

"Yes, I know," Boaz replied. "But I also know about everything you have done for your mother-in-law since the death of your husband. I have heard how you left your father and mother and your own land to live here among complete strangers. May the LORD, the God of Israel, under whose wings you have come to take refuge, reward you fully for what you have done." . . .

So Ruth told her mother-in-law about the man in whose field she had worked. She said, "The man I worked with today is named Boaz."

"May the LORD bless him!" Naomi told her daughter-in-law. "He is showing his **kindness** to us as well as to your dead husband. That man is one of our closest relatives, one of our family redeemers."

Hebrew *hesed*; see today's word study.

UNEXPECTED BLESSINGS

[Ruth] loves you and has been better to you than seven sons!

RUTH 4:15

Naomi and Ruth came together in less-than-ideal circumstances. To escape a famine in Israel, Naomi's family moved to Moab. While living there, her two sons married Moabite women: Orpah and Ruth. Then Naomi's husband and sons died. In that culture, women were dependent on men, which left the three widows in a predicament.

Word came to Naomi that the famine in Israel had ended, so she decided to make the long trek home. Orpah and Ruth started to go with her, but Naomi urged them to return home, saying, "The hand of the LORD has gone out against me" (Ruth 1:13 ESV).

Orpah went home, but Ruth continued, affirming her belief in Naomi's God despite Naomi's own fragile faith (vv. 15–18).

The story started in desperately unpleasant circumstances: famine, death, and despair (vv. 1–5). It changed direction due to undeserved kindnesses: Ruth to Naomi (vv. 16–17; 2:11–12) and Boaz to Ruth (vv. 13–14).

It involved unlikely people: two widows (an aging Jew and a young gentile) and Boaz, the son of a prostitute (Joshua 2:1; Matthew 1:5).

It depended on unexplainable intervention: Ruth just so "happened" to glean in the field of Boaz (Ruth 2:3).

And it ended in unimaginable blessing: a baby who would be in the lineage of the Messiah (4:16–17; Matthew 1:5–16).

God makes miracles out of what seems insignificant: fragile faith, a little kindness, and ordinary people.

—Julie Ackerman Link

When have you experienced unexpected, unearned kindness from someone? How did it feel to receive their compassion?

_____

_____

_____

_____

_____

_____

_____

How can you encourage, support, or serve someone in your life?

_____

_____

_____

_____

_____

_____

Word Study

STEADFAST LOVE [NLT translation—*kindness*]
hesed (Ruth 2:20)

One of the most significant words for love in Scripture is the Hebrew word *hesed*. This word, sometimes translated "steadfast love," identifies love that is unconditionally faithful. It's fiercely loyal love that isn't earned by its recipient but flows naturally from the character of the giver.

Although there are only a few explicit mentions of the word *hesed* in the book of Ruth (which the NLT translates "kindness" in 1:8 and 2:20 and "family loyalty" in 3:10), the story told in Ruth is itself a case study of *hesed*—faithful love—demonstrated in the harshest of circumstances. Ruth's faithful, unconditional love and care for her mother-in-law—long after she was obligated to (1:11–14)—is the book's central example of *hesed*. As celebrated in Psalm 136, such faithful human love points to God's *hesed*, which endures forever (vv. 1–26).

ENGAGE

Identify times—both significant and ordinary—where God was faithfully leading, guiding, and directing your steps, as He did in Ruth's life circumstances.

- _____
- _____
- _____
- _____
- _____
- _____
- _____
- _____
- _____
- _____
- _____

I praise and thank You for the way
You've always carried me. In Jesus's name, amen.

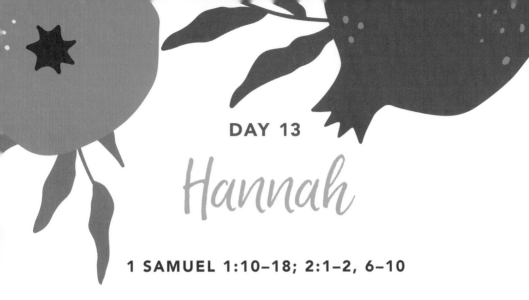

DAY 13

Hannah

1 SAMUEL 1:10–18; 2:1–2, 6–10

Hannah was in deep anguish, crying bitterly as she prayed to the LORD. And she made **this vow**: "O LORD of Heaven's Armies, if you will look upon my sorrow and answer my prayer and give me a son, then I will give him back to you. He will be yours for his entire lifetime, and as a sign that he has been dedicated to the LORD, his hair will never be cut."

> The prayer that follows is Hannah's prayer of lament (1:11).

As she was praying to the LORD, Eli watched her. Seeing her lips moving but hearing no sound, he thought she had been drinking. "Must you come here drunk?" he demanded. "Throw away your wine!"

"Oh no, sir!" she replied. "I haven't been drinking wine or anything stronger. But I am very discouraged, and I was pouring out my heart to the LORD. Don't think I am a wicked woman! For I have been praying out of great anguish and sorrow."

"In that case," Eli said, "go in peace! May the God of Israel grant the request you have asked of him."

"Oh, thank you, sir!" she exclaimed. Then she went back and began to eat again, and she was no longer sad. . . .

Then Hannah **prayed**:

The prayer that follows is Hannah's prayer of praise (2:1–2, 6–10).

"My heart rejoices in the LORD!
  The LORD has made me strong.
Now I have an answer for my enemies;
  I rejoice because you rescued me.
No one is holy like the LORD!
  There is no one besides you;
  there is no Rock like our God. . . .

"The LORD gives both death and life;
  he brings some down to the grave but raises others up.
The LORD makes some poor and others rich;
  he brings some down and lifts others up.
He lifts the poor from the dust
  and the needy from the garbage dump.
He sets them among princes,
  placing them in seats of honor.
For all the earth is the LORD's,
  and he has set the world in order.

"He will protect his faithful ones,
  but the wicked will disappear in darkness.
No one will succeed by strength alone.
  Those who fight against the LORD will be shattered.
He thunders against them from heaven;
  the LORD judges throughout the earth.
He gives power to his king;
  he increases the strength of his anointed one."

RENEWED VISION

**My heart rejoices in the LORD! The LORD has
made me strong.**

1 SAMUEL 2:1

After a painful minor surgery on my left eye, my doctor recommended a vision test. With confidence, I covered my right eye and read each line on the chart with ease. Covering my left eye, I gasped. How could I not realize I'd been so blind?

While adjusting to new glasses and renewed vision, I thought of how daily trials often caused me to be spiritually nearsighted. Focusing only on what I could see up-close—my pain and ever-changing circumstances—I became blind to the faithfulness of my eternal and unchanging God. With such a limited perspective, hope became an unattainable blur.

First Samuel 1 tells the story of another woman who failed to recognize God's trustworthiness while focusing on her current anguish, uncertainty, and loss. For years, Hannah had endured childlessness and endless torment from Peninnah, the other wife of her husband Elkanah. Hannah's husband adored her, but contentment evaded her. One day, she prayed with bitter honesty. When Eli the priest questioned her, she explained her situation. As she left, he prayed that God would grant her request (v. 17). Though Hannah's situation didn't change immediately, she walked away with confident hope (v. 18).

Her prayer in 1 Samuel 2:1–2 reveals a shift in Hannah's focus. Even before her circumstances improved, Hannah's renewed vision changed her perspective and her attitude. She rejoiced in the ongoing presence of God—her Rock and everlasting hope.

—Xochitl Dixon

PROFILE: HANNAH

Hannah's story is set in one of the darkest eras of Israel's history, the period when the judges ruled. A time of violence, invasions by powerful enemies, and idol worship. But in 1 Samuel 1–2, we discover Hannah has committed herself to the one true God. Each year, she and her family traveled to the tabernacle to worship (1:3). And recorded through her prayers is the evidence that she believed God's love and concern extended not only to God's collective people—the nation of Israel—but to her, personally.

To Hannah, God was both powerful and present (1:11; 2:10): the one moved by, and able to respond to, her personal needs, griefs, and desires. Hannah's bold outpouring of praise in 1 Samuel 2 likely influenced what is known as the Magnificat, Mary's song of praise recorded in Luke 1.

How does focusing on God's unchanging nature instead of your circumstances give you greater hope?

_____

_____

_____

_____

_____

_____

Where are you currently struggling with spiritual nearsightedness? Tell God about your struggle, listening for His loving response to you.

_____

_____

_____

_____

_____

_____

ENGAGE

Choose either Hannah's prayer of lament (1 Samuel 1:10–11) or her prayer of praise (1 Samuel 2:1–2, 6–10), and make it your own. Write your own lament or song of praise, voicing needs, joys, or heartaches, or declaring God's majesty, creativity, or boundless love.

DAY 14

Abigail

1 SAMUEL 25:3, 14, 17–26, 30–32

This man's name was Nabal, and his wife, Abigail, was a sensible and beautiful woman. But Nabal, a descendant of Caleb, was crude and mean in all his dealings. . . .

One of Nabal's servants went to Abigail and told her, "David sent messengers from the wilderness to greet our master, but [Nabal] screamed insults at them. . . . You need to know this and figure out what to do, for there is going to be trouble for our master and his whole family. He's so ill-tempered that no one can even talk to him!"

Abigail wasted no time. She quickly gathered 200 loaves of bread, two wineskins full of wine, five sheep that had been slaughtered, nearly a bushel of roasted grain, 100 clusters of raisins, and 200 fig cakes. She packed them on donkeys and said to her servants, "Go on ahead. I will follow you shortly." But she didn't tell her husband Nabal what she was doing.

As she was riding her donkey into a mountain ravine, she saw David and his men coming toward her. David had just been saying, "A lot of good it did to help this fellow. We protected his flocks in the wilderness, and nothing he owned was lost or stolen. But he has repaid me evil for good. May God strike me and kill me if even one man of his household is still alive tomorrow morning!"

When Abigail saw David, she quickly got off her donkey and bowed low before him. She fell at his feet and said, "I accept all blame in this matter, my lord. Please listen to what I have to say. I know Nabal is a wicked and ill-tempered man; please don't pay any attention to him. He is a fool, just as his name suggests. But I never even saw the young men you sent.

"Now, my lord, as surely as the LORD lives and you yourself live, since the LORD has kept you from murdering and taking vengeance into your own hands, let all your enemies and those who try to harm you be as cursed as Nabal is. . . .

"When the LORD has done all he promised and has made you leader of Israel, don't let this be a blemish on your record. Then your conscience won't have to bear the staggering burden of needless bloodshed and vengeance. And when the LORD has done these great things for you, please remember me, your servant!"

David replied to Abigail, "Praise the LORD, the God of Israel, who has sent you to meet me today!"

HARD CONVERSATIONS

**"When the LORD has done all he promised and has made you
leader of Israel, don't let this be a blemish on your record,"
[Abigail told David].**

1 SAMUEL 25:30–31

I once drove fifty miles to have a hard conversation with a remote staff
person. I had received a report from another employee that suggested
he was misrepresenting our company, and I was concerned for our reputation. I felt nudged to offer an opinion that might change his choices.

In 1 Samuel 25, an unlikely person took great personal risk to confront a
future king of Israel who was about to make a disastrous choice. Abigail
was married to Nabal, whose character matched the meaning of his
name ("fool") (vv. 3, 25). Nabal had refused to pay David and his troops
the customary wage for protecting his livestock (vv. 10–11). Hearing
that David planned a murderous revenge on her household, and knowing her foolish husband wouldn't listen to reason, Abigail prepared a
peace offering, rode to meet David, and persuaded him to reconsider
(vv. 18–31).

How did Abigail accomplish this? After sending ahead donkeys loaded
with food to satisfy David and his men and settle the debt, she spoke
truth to David. She wisely reminded David of God's call on his life. If he
resisted his desire for revenge, when God made him king, he wouldn't
"have on his conscience the staggering burden of needless bloodshed"
(v. 31 NIV).

You might also know someone dangerously close to a mistake that
could harm others and compromise their own future effectiveness for
God. Like Abigail, might God be calling you to a hard conversation?

—Elisa Morgan

Is God inviting you to engage in a hard conversation? What fears or obstacles are blocking you from following through?

_____

_____

_____

_____

_____

_____

What do you need as you ready yourself for that conversation? Share with God what you need. How does He lovingly respond to you?

_____

_____

_____

_____

_____

_____

_____

_____

POMEGRANATES, OLIVE OIL, AND HONEY . . .

If you lived in ancient Israel, yours was a primarily plant-based diet. Harvested from your own fields, wheat and barley would be transformed into bread and roasted grains, and lentils into stews. By contrast, meat was a special treat. Festivals and the occasion of having a guest (see Genesis 18:7–8; 1 Samuel 28:24–25) were some of the few times you would have gone to the great lengths of slaughtering a prized goat, sheep, or cow from your costly herd. Dairy products—such as milk, cheese, and yogurt—would supplement your vegetarian diet.

Deuteronomy 8:8 lists "seven species" that formed the plant-based staples of an Israelite's diet. They were "wheat and barley, vines and fig trees, pomegranates, olive oil and honey" (NIV). We see several of the seven in the food provisions Abigail brings to David and his mighty men: bread, wine, grain, raisins, and fig cakes (1 Samuel 25:18).

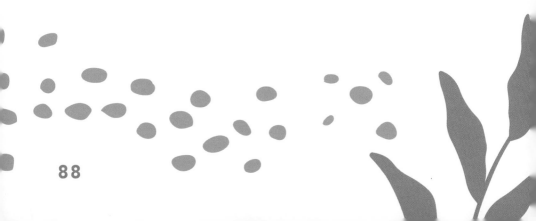

ENGAGE

Read 1 Samuel 25 a second time. What part of Abigail's story seems to be speaking directly to your heart? Give yourself space to reflect on that part of the story along with God. If you're feeling stuck, ask Him, What do you want me to learn in this story?

DAY 15

Bathsheba

2 SAMUEL 11:2–5, 27; 12:1–10, 24–25

Late one afternoon, after his midday rest, David got out of bed and was walking on the roof of the palace. As he looked out over the city, he noticed a woman of unusual beauty taking a bath. He sent someone to find out who she was, and he was told, "She is Bathsheba, the daughter of Eliam and the wife of Uriah the Hittite." Then David sent messengers to get her; and when she came to the palace, he slept with her. She had just completed the purification rites after having her menstrual period. Then she returned home. Later, when Bathsheba discovered that she was pregnant, she sent David a message, saying, "I'm pregnant." . . .

The LORD was displeased with what David had done.

So the LORD sent Nathan the prophet to tell David this story: "There were two men in a certain town. One was rich, and one was poor. The rich man owned a great many sheep and cattle. The poor man owned nothing but one little lamb he had bought. He raised that little lamb, and it grew up with his children. It ate from the man's own plate and drank from his cup. He cuddled it in his arms like a baby daughter. One day a guest arrived at the home of the rich man. But instead of killing an animal from his own flock or herd, he took the poor man's lamb and killed it and prepared it for his guest."

David was furious. "As surely as the LORD lives," he vowed, "any man who would do such a thing deserves to die! He must repay four lambs to the poor man for the one he stole and for having no pity."

Then Nathan said to David, "You are that man! The LORD, the God of Israel, says: I anointed you king of Israel and saved you from the power of Saul. I gave you your master's house and his wives and the kingdoms of Israel and Judah. And if that had not been enough, I would have given you much, much more. Why, then, have you despised the word of the LORD and done this horrible deed? For you have murdered Uriah the Hittite with the sword of the Ammonites and stolen his wife. From this time on, your family will live by the sword because you have despised me by taking Uriah's wife to be your own." . . .

Then David comforted Bathsheba, his wife, and slept with her. She became pregnant and gave birth to a son, and David named him Solomon. The LORD loved the child and sent word through Nathan the prophet that they should name him Jedidiah (which means "beloved of the LORD"), as the LORD had commanded.

NEVER OVERLOOKED

She gave birth to a son, and they named him Solomon.

2 SAMUEL 12:24 NIV

When a youth group discussed the story of Bathsheba, a student asked if King David's misuse of power could be called sexual assault. The leader replied no, and one of Rachael Denhollander's friends added that Bathsheba was at fault because "she could have chosen to die rather than have sex with him." Those words hit Rachael deeply, because she had been sexually abused by her US Olympics' gymnastics coach. "This . . . told me I would be better off dead than a rape victim."*

In contrast, the biblical account places the blame on David: "The LORD was displeased with what David had done" (2 Samuel 11:27); the prophet Nathan also pointed the finger at David (see 12:7–10). Although David was in the wrong, God brought forth redemption and saved Bathsheba from disgrace. David married Bathsheba, which in that context would have kept her from being marginalized, as was so often the case for widows. God blessed them with a son, Solomon, who became a wise king. God didn't overlook her; she was known and loved by Him.

God too knows the gymnast Rachael. Over the years she wrestled with Scripture to understand His view of abuse. She trusts in God to mete out justice and calls evil for what it is, "because God is good and holy."† If we've experienced the horrors of abuse, and if we haven't, we can believe that God knows us and works for our restoration and flourishing.

—Amy Boucher Pye

---

*Kimi Harris, "Time Doesn't Heal Sexual Assault If Victims Are Silenced," *Christianity Today*, October 8, 2018, https://www.christianitytoday.com/ct/2018/october-web-only/sexual-abuse-trama-victims-silenced-rachael-denhollander.html.

†Morgan Lee, "My Larry Nassar Testimony Went Viral.," *Christianity Today*, January 31, 2018, https://www.christianitytoday.com/ct/2018/january-web-only/rachael-denhollander-larry-nassar-forgiveness-gospel.html.

When you've experienced some kind of wrongdoing, how have you looked to God for a resolution? How can you come before Him today with all your thoughts and feelings?

BATHSHEBA'S DEFENSE

Was Bathsheba guilty? Many suggest that Bathsheba was seducing or at least willingly partnering with David in adultery. But the Bible portrays her story very differently. God—through the prophet Nathan—identified Bathsheba as a victim of abuse (2 Samuel 12:1–15). God comes to Bathsheba's defense, implicating David through Nathan's parable: In the tale, a rich man owned many sheep, but a poor man had just one—a beloved ewe lamb that he cherished like a "daughter" (v. 3). The rich man "killed it and prepared it for his guest" (v. 4). In Nathan's accusation, Bathsheba is compared to this slaughtered lamb, and David to the man who butchered her (v. 4). And for David's brutality God takes it upon Himself to bring David to justice.

In modern terms, David's assault would be *power rape*. That is, David abused his power by sexually victimizing Bathsheba, someone vulnerable—helpless—in the face of David's absolute authority. Statutory rape is another way to label David's sexual assault. Often seen as having sex with minors, *statutory rape* occurs when the victim is underage or incapable of freely consenting, due to the offender's power over him or her.

ENGAGE

Identify an area of your life where you are still healing from betrayal, disappointment, loss, mistreatment, or abuse. Imagine that you are at your kitchen table (or whatever space is most comfortable), sitting across from Jesus. Share with Him about your pain. Feel His protective love for you while He listens attentively. Tell Him what you need at this stage in your healing journey.

Rizpah

2 SAMUEL 21:1–2, 4–14

There was a famine during David's reign that lasted for three years, so David asked the LORD about it. And the LORD said, "The famine has come because Saul and his family are guilty of murdering the Gibeonites."

So the king summoned the Gibeonites. . . .

"What can I do then?" David asked. "Just tell me and I will do it for you."

Then they replied, "It was Saul who planned to destroy us, to keep us from having any place at all in the territory of Israel. So let seven of Saul's sons be handed over to us, and we will execute them before the LORD at Gibeon, on the mountain of the LORD."

"All right," the king said, "I will do it." The king spared Jonathan's son Mephibosheth, who was Saul's grandson, because of the oath David and Jonathan had sworn before the LORD. But he gave them Saul's two sons Armoni and Mephibosheth, whose mother was Rizpah daughter of Aiah. He also gave them the five sons of Saul's daughter Merab, the wife of Adriel son of Barzillai from Meholah. The men of Gibeon executed them on the mountain before the LORD. So all seven of them died together at the beginning of the barley harvest.

Then Rizpah daughter of Aiah, the mother of two of the men, spread burlap on a rock and stayed there the entire harvest season. She prevented the scavenger birds from tearing at their bodies during the day and stopped wild animals from eating them at night. When David learned what Rizpah, Saul's concubine, had done, he went to the people of Jabesh-gilead and retrieved the bones of Saul and his son Jonathan. (When the Philistines had killed Saul and Jonathan on Mount Gilboa, the people of Jabesh-gilead stole their bodies from the public square of Beth-shan, where the Philistines had hung them.) So David obtained the bones of Saul and Jonathan, as well as the bones of the men the Gibeonites had executed.

Then the king ordered that they bury the bones in the tomb of Kish, Saul's father, at the town of Zela in the land of Benjamin. After that, God ended the famine in the land.

SIT DOWN

**Rizpah . . . took sackcloth and spread it out
for herself on a rock.**

2 SAMUEL 21:10 NIV

Sarah's parents became addicted to drugs and chose them over caring for her as she needed. She was taken away from them and given to a couple who started selling her to men. At twelve, she had her first baby. Adding to that grief, her baby died. She felt used, invisible, powerless, traumatized.

Perhaps Sarah knew some of Rizpah's pain (2 Samuel 21:1–14). The concubine, or "second wife," of King Saul, bore him two sons. When he was killed, the land was in famine and the new king, David, asked God why. He said it was because King Saul had put the Gibeonites to death (v. 1). So David let the Gibeonites hang the king's seven sons, including Rizpah's two (v. 9). She was powerless to stop this tragedy. For the sake of love, Rizpah mustered the courage to guard her sons' bodies from birds and beasts (v. 10). From spring to fall, she sat, protecting their decaying bodies. When David heard about her loyalty, he had their bodies gathered for burial (vv. 11–13). This must have brought Rizpah a little peace.

When Sarah was a young adult, God placed a new friend in her life. She gained the courage to share her painful story, and slowly she received God's love in Christ as her own. Still the past trauma causes nightmares. What brings her the most hope? That friend sits with her in her pain and prays. One day total healing for all of us will come. But in the meantime, let's sit down with others and listen to their stories.

—Anne Cetas

If you've suffered trauma or abuse, or even something that feels too small to be called that but still causes you pain, ask God what you should do about that. Is there someone safe with whom you should share your story? What healing needs to occur?

_____

_____

_____

_____

_____

_____

_____

_____

_____

_____

_____

Follow-up: Is there someone for whom you can be the listener? Ask God to open your eyes to others' pain.

BURIAL AND DEATH

In ancient Israel, you honored your loved ones, not just in life but in death. That is, to "honor your father and mother," as the fifth command-ment said (Exodus 20:12), included providing them a proper burial.

Improper burial was the ultimate dishonor—sometimes considered a divine curse against you or your family. Take the case of the infamous Queen Jezebel, whose body, Elijah prophesied, would not be buried but be eaten by dogs (1 Kings 21:23). An ordinary—if ghastly—formula for cursing someone in the ancient Near East was this: pronouncing that their unburied corpse would be scavenged by vultures or wild ani-mals, or both (see examples in Deuteronomy 28:26; 1 Samuel 17:44, 46; Jeremiah 7:33; 15:3).

In today's Bible passage, Rizpah contested that fate for her deceased sons. In all weather, she guarded their bodies, chasing away "scaven-ger birds" and "wild animals," until their bones were properly buried (2 Samuel 21:10). God honored her for her worthy act of providing dig-nity for the deceased: once David properly buried the bones of Saul's family, including those of Rizpah's sons, in response to her vigil, God ended the famine (v. 14).

ENGAGE

Imagine yourself present to Rizpah's story. View the setting in your mind's eye, taking in the hour of day, the weather. Where do you find yourself in the scene? Pay attention to Rizpah as she keeps watch over the bodies of her sons, night and day. What do you want to tell her? What does she want you to know?

DAY 17

Queen of Sheba

1 KINGS 10:1–10, 13; MATTHEW 12:38–39, 42

When the queen of Sheba heard of Solomon's fame, which brought honor to the name of the LORD, she came to test him with hard questions. She arrived in Jerusalem with a large group of attendants and a great caravan of camels loaded with spices, large quantities of gold, and precious jewels. When she met with Solomon, she talked with him about everything she had on her mind. Solomon had answers for all her questions; nothing was too hard for the king to explain to her. When the queen of Sheba realized how very wise Solomon was, and when she saw the palace he had built, she was overwhelmed. She was also amazed at the food on his tables, the organization of his officials and their splendid clothing, the cup-bearers, and the burnt offerings Solomon made at the Temple of the LORD.

She exclaimed to the king, "Everything I heard in my country about your achievements and wisdom is true! I didn't believe what was said until I arrived here and saw it with my own eyes. In fact, I had not heard the half of it! Your wisdom and prosperity are far beyond what I was told. How happy your people must be! What a privilege for your officials to stand here day after day, listening to your wisdom! Praise the LORD your God, who delights in you and has placed you on the throne of Israel. Because of the LORD's eternal love for Israel, he has made you king so you can rule with justice and righteousness."

Then she gave the king a gift of 9,000 pounds of gold, great quantities of spices, and precious jewels. Never again were so many spices brought in as those the queen of Sheba gave to King Solomon. . . .

King Solomon gave the queen of Sheba whatever she asked for, besides all the customary gifts he had so generously given. Then she and all her attendants returned to their own land.

One day some teachers of religious law and Pharisees came to Jesus and said, "Teacher, we want you to show us a miraculous sign to prove your authority."

But Jesus replied, . . . "The queen of Sheba will also stand up against this generation on judgment day and condemn it, for she came from a distant land to hear the wisdom of Solomon. Now someone greater than Solomon is here—but you refuse to listen."

STANDING ROYALLY FOR CHRIST

The Queen of the South will rise at the judgment.

MATTHEW 12:42 NIV

She was dark. Lovely, too. That's almost certainly true of the queen of Sheba, the renowned female monarch who traveled with her great caravan to Jerusalem to test King Solomon's famed wisdom. An admirable quest, her visit became legendary when, as a pagan queen from Sheba or Saba—possibly Ethiopia, or modern-day Yemen—this intriguing ruler credited Solomon's wealth and wisdom to his God:

"Praise the LORD your God, who delights in you and has placed you on the throne of Israel. Because of the LORD's eternal love for Israel, he has made you king so you can rule with justice and righteousness" (1 Kings 10:9).

Her stunning acknowledgement, sadly, is often overlooked by ongoing controversy regarding the queen. Some doubt she existed, or question her ethnicity—saying she wasn't African or Arabian—calling her "just" an allegory of how the world's unbelievers will one day submit to heaven's God. Her struggle to be seen in history as a real person of worth should rally any of us whose value or credentials have been doubted. Stand tall anyway.

To Christ Himself, indeed, the "Queen of the South," as He referred to her, displayed such godly regard that she will "rise at the judgment with this generation and condemn it; for she came from the ends of the earth to listen to Solomon's wisdom, and now something greater than Solomon is here" (Matthew 12:42 NIV). Pharisees had doubted Jesus, asking Him to prove Himself with signs. Instead, Jesus says seek Him as Sheba's queen sought wisdom. Her example inspires still.

—Patricia Raybon

104

How do you feel when someone doubts all that you are—as they did and still do with Jesus and the queen of Sheba?

_____

_____

_____

_____

_____

When Jesus affirms the queen of Sheba, what is He saying about the potential for any of us—including you and me—to play a key role in His kingdom?

_____

_____

_____

_____

_____

_____

PROFILE: QUEEN OF SHEBA

The larger-than-life queen of Sheba arrived in style at Solomon's court, and then abruptly exited. Who was this bold, brilliant, mysterious queen? She was powerful: ruler of an influential kingdom in Arabia or Ethiopia. Queens from Arabia are memorialized in Assyrian records, and queens from Ethiopia are mentioned in the Bible (Acts 8:27), by other ancient historians, and in Ethiopian tradition. For example, in Ethiopia's founding story, the queen of Sheba had a son with Solomon, from whom the royal dynasty descended.

She was also likely fabulously rich: the ancient kingdom of Sheba in Arabia, if she did indeed hail from there as historians today suspect, overflowed with wealth through its control of trade routes for myrrh, frankincense, and gold. Ethiopia was also affluent. As a premier leader of a kingdom built on trade and wealth, she was akin to the CEO of Sheba. In 1 Kings, this charismatic, wise queen was likely on business: testing not only Solomon's wisdom but also his potential as a trade partner.

ENGAGE

Jesus honored the queen of Sheba for her persistence—for her relentless pursuit of wisdom from "the ends of the earth" (Matthew 12:42 NIV). In what way is God calling you to persist in carrying out a responsibility, gift, or vocation He's given to you, no matter how unglamorous or unseen it is?

Whether your efforts include pressing into that tough job, relationship, or cause, or simply folding the laundry for the millionth time, tell God that you want to be faithful to what He's entrusted to you.

_____

_____

_____

_____

_____

_____

_____

_____

_____

_____

_____

_____

Widow at Zarephath

1 KINGS 17:8–16

Then the LORD said to Elijah, "Go and live in the village of Zarephath, near the city of Sidon. I have instructed a widow there to feed you."

So he went to Zarephath. As he arrived at the gates of the village, he saw a widow gathering sticks, and he asked her, "Would you please bring me a little water in a cup?" As she was going to get it, he called to her, "Bring me a bite of bread, too."

But she said, "I swear by the LORD your God that I don't have a single piece of bread in the house. And I have only a handful of flour left in the jar and a little cooking oil in the bottom of the jug. I was just gathering a few sticks to cook this last meal, and then my son and I will die."

But Elijah said to her, "Don't be afraid! Go ahead and do just what you've said, but make a little bread for me first. Then use what's left to prepare a meal for yourself and your son. For this is what the LORD, the God of Israel, says: There will always be flour and olive oil left in your containers until the time when the LORD sends rain and the crops grow again!"

So she did as Elijah said, and she and Elijah and her family continued to eat for many days. There was always enough flour and olive oil left in the containers, just as the LORD had promised through Elijah.

FACING THE FUTURE

Elijah said to her, "Don't be afraid!"

1 KINGS 17:13

The widow had almost certainly worn the weight of dread like a heavy cloak for some time. The extended drought and famine were about to make her worst fears come true. She planned to kindle a fire and cook the last of her food. After that, she and her son would starve. As she was gathering sticks, a prophet approached and asked for some bread and water. Did he notice what I imagine were her tear-filled eyes, the worry lines on her face, her trembling hands?

"Don't be afraid!" Elijah said (1 Kings 17:13). He assured her she'd have enough flour and oil to survive until God sent rain (v. 14). God had seen her situation and would provide for her family and His prophet. Eventually, the weight of the widow's anxiety lifted, but it must have returned when her son died. What deep grief she must have experienced! And, without him, she'd be helpless in her old age. Again, God reached into her life and enabled Elijah to resurrect the boy. These experiences almost certainly established her faith in the one true God (v. 24).

Many of us feel anxiety amidst loss, dwindling resources, and uncertainty. As was likely the case for the widow, our fear can become a gateway for faith—faith in the God of hope (Romans 15:13). We don't have to fear the future because God sees our needs. We can grow closer to Him as we depend on His loving care.

—Jennifer Benson Schuldt

What is your greatest fear today? How does it help to know that God sees you and loves you?

_____

_____

_____

_____

_____

ENGAGE

Read 1 Kings 17:8–16 a second time, slowly. _Listen_ deeply, allowing God to speak to your mind and heart as you read. Does anything from the passage stand out to you? Or, what might God be inviting you to through the Scripture passage? Journal about your experience.

_____

_____

_____

_____

_____

_____

FAMILY NUTRITION IN THE ANCIENT WORLD

What worried parents in the ancient world? Food security was a constant anxiety. Unlike today, you couldn't buy diverse, nutrient-dense vegetables or meat from your local grocery store. Refrigeration for animal-based products, like milk, wasn't available. (Except when your livestock had young, you didn't have milk at all.)

For most of the year, diets lacked diversity: Kids in ancient Israel hardly ate any vegetables and very little meat, and, as a result, had severe vitamin and mineral deficiencies (such as iron, calcium, and vitamins A and C).* There were years of bountiful harvests. But everyone suffered in times of crop shortages and famine, as we see in today's story about the widow of Zarephath and her son.

Children suffered most of all: in ancient Israelite households, most parents would have about six children, and only two or three would reach adulthood.†

---

*Carol Meyers, *Rediscovering Eve: Ancient Israelite Women in Context* (Oxford: Oxford University Press, 2013), 53–58, 98–99.
†Meyers, *Rediscovering Eve*, 98–99.

DAY 19

Widow of the Prophet

2 KINGS 4:1–7

One day the widow of a member of the group of prophets came to Elisha and cried out, "My husband who served you is dead, and you know how he feared the LORD. But now a creditor has come, threatening to take my two sons as slaves."

"What can I do to help you?" Elisha asked. "Tell me, what do you have in the house?"

"Nothing at all, except a flask of olive oil," she replied.

And Elisha said, "Borrow as many empty jars as you can from your friends and neighbors. Then go into your house with your sons and shut the door behind you. Pour olive oil from your flask into the jars, setting each one aside when it is filled."

So she did as she was told. Her sons kept bringing jars to her, and she filled one after another. Soon every container was full to the brim!

"Bring me another jar," she said to one of her sons.

"There aren't any more!" he told her. And then the olive oil stopped flowing.

When she told the man of God what had happened, he said to her, "Now sell the olive oil and pay your debts, and you and your sons can live on what is left over."

THE WIDOW'S FAITH

Your heavenly Father already knows all your needs.

MATTHEW 6:32

It is pitch dark when Ah-pi starts her day. Others in the village will wake up soon to make their way to the rubber plantation. Harvesting latex is one of the main sources of income for people living in Hongzhuang Village, China. To collect as much latex as possible, the trees must be tapped very early in the morning, before daybreak. Ah-pi will be among the rubber tappers, but first she will spend time communing with God.

Ah-pi's father, husband, and only son have passed away, and she—with her daughter-in-law—is providing for an elderly mother and two young grandsons. Her story reminds me of another widow in the Bible who trusted God.

The widow's husband had died and left her in debt (2 Kings 4:1). In her distress, she looked to God for help by turning to His servant Elisha. She believed that God cared and that He could do something about her situation. And God did. He provided miraculously for the dire needs of this widow (vv. 5–6). This same God also provided for Ah-pi—though less miraculously—through the toil of her hands, the produce from the ground, and gifts from His people.

Though life can make various demands on us, we can always draw strength from God. We can entrust our cares to Him, do all we can, and let Him amaze us with what He can do with our situation.

—Poh Fang Chia

Has God ever provided for you or someone you know in an amazing way?
Praise God for His provision.

_____

_____

_____

_____

_____

Where do you need God to move on your behalf? Talk with Him about it.

_____

_____

_____

_____

_____

_____

_____

_____

OLIVE OIL

It might surprise us that large quantities of olive oil would be enough to entirely reverse the widow's financial hardship (2 Kings 4:7). But olive oil was central to daily life in Israel, used for cooking, medicine, light, sacrifices, and other religious ceremonies such as anointing kings and priests. Olive oil was also a primary trade resource and could be used as currency (see, for example, 1 Kings 5:8–11).

Olive oil was deeply significant to Israel as a symbol of God's provision of a "good land" rich in "olive oil and honey . . . where food is plentiful and nothing is lacking" (Deuteronomy 8:8–9). Yet such flourishing is connected to Israel's faithfulness (vv. 11–19). The widow's dwindling oil would have been a poignant example of the way in which those most economically vulnerable—widows and orphans—suffer when God's people fail to care for and provide for them. In Deuteronomy 24:17–20, for example, Israel is given explicit instructions to ensure olive oil is provided for widows and orphans. In reversing the widow's fortunes, God revealed Himself as the one who advocates for those uncared for by society so "that orphans and widows receive justice" (10:18).

ENGAGE

In 2 Kings 4:2, the prophet Elisha asked the widow, "Tell me, what do you have?" God then miraculously provided for her and her entire family through what was already in her house—olive oil! Today you may be facing challenges. An overwhelming situation. Ask God what He's already put into your hands to take the next step in facing your situation or circumstances, and then journal about your conversation with God and the resource you already have.

We can entrust
our cares to God, do
all we can, and let
Him amaze us with
what He can do
with our situation.

DAY 20

Shunammite Woman

2 KINGS 4:8–21, 32–37

One day Elisha went to the town of Shunem. A wealthy woman lived there, and she urged him to come to her home for a meal. After that, whenever he passed that way, he would stop there for something to eat.

She said to her husband, "I am sure this man who stops in from time to time is a holy man of God. Let's build a small room for him on the roof and furnish it with a bed, a table, a chair, and a lamp. Then he will have a place to stay whenever he comes by."

One day Elisha returned to Shunem, and he went up to this upper room to rest. He said to his servant Gehazi, "Tell the woman from Shunem I want to speak to her." When she appeared, Elisha said to Gehazi, "Tell her, 'We appreciate the kind concern you have shown us. What can we do for you? Can we put in a good word for you to the king or to the commander of the army?'"

"No," she replied, "my family takes good care of me."

Later Elisha asked Gehazi, "What can we do for her?"

Gehazi replied, "She doesn't have a son, and her husband is an old man."

"Call her back again," Elisha told him. When the woman returned, Elisha said to her as she stood in the doorway, "Next year at this time you will be holding a son in your arms!"

"No, my lord!" she cried. "O man of God, don't deceive me and get my hopes up like that."

But sure enough, the woman soon became pregnant. And at that time the following year she had a son, just as Elisha had said.

One day when her child was older, he went out to help his father, who was working with the harvesters. Suddenly he cried out, "My head hurts! My head hurts!"

His father said to one of the servants, "Carry him home to his mother."

So the servant took him home, and his mother held him on her lap. But around noontime he died. She carried him up and laid him on the bed of the man of God, then shut the door and left him there. . . .

When Elisha arrived, the child was indeed dead, lying there on the prophet's bed. He went in alone and shut the door behind him and prayed to the LORD. Then he lay down on the child's body, placing his mouth on the child's mouth, his eyes on the child's eyes, and his hands on the child's hands. And as he stretched out on him, the child's body began to grow warm again! Elisha got up, walked back and forth across the room once, and then stretched himself out again on the child. This time the boy sneezed seven times and opened his eyes!

Then Elisha summoned Gehazi. "Call the child's mother!" he said. And when she came in, Elisha said, "Here, take your son!" She fell at his feet and bowed before him, overwhelmed with gratitude. Then she took her son in her arms and carried him downstairs.

UNNAMED BUT NOT UNNOTICED

Whatever you do, work at it with all your heart, as working for the Lord, not for human masters.

COLOSSIANS 3:23 NIV

Colleen had spent weeks planning the children's Christmas program at church, but when the pastor thanked people on the night of the event, he failed to mention her. Colleen hadn't expected much, but to be forgotten completely stung a little.

In 2 Kings 4, we read about the prophet Elisha. Whenever he came to Shunem, a local woman invited him for a meal. She then observed that Elisha didn't have anywhere to stay and suggested she and her husband could build an extra room in their house for him. The man of God was grateful and revealed to her that she would soon have a son (vv. 8–17). In the years that followed, Elisha continued to be a valuable friend when the family faced a life-and-death situation (vv. 18–37).

It's interesting that we never learn the name of the Shunammite woman. Some translations just call her "a great woman" (4:8) And so she was. Throughout her life, she seemed great in faith, in hospitality, and in service to God, whom she loved and worshipped.

Although we don't always receive acknowledgment for the things we do, we know when we commit our work to the Lord that He sees us even if no one else notices.

Though the woman of Shunem remains unnamed, her acts of service didn't go unnoticed by God. God knew His child as someone who desired with her whole heart to please Him (Colossians 3:23).

—Cindy Hess Kasper

Talk to God about times when you feel unnoticed or underappreciated.

_____

_____

_____

_____

_____

_____

Ask God to show you just how much He loves you.

_____

_____

_____

_____

_____

_____

_____

EDUCATION AND LITERACY

> Make sure your children learn [these commandments].
> Talk about them when you are at home. Talk about them
> when you walk along the road. Speak about them when
> you go to bed. And speak about them when you get up.
> (Deuteronomy 6:7 NIrV)

Homeschooling was probably your only education option in ancient Israel. Schools, if they did exist before the sixth century BC, were for the aristocracy. In most families, a child was apprenticed in the skills of his or her parents: a girl in the crafts of bread baking, weaving, and pottery making, and a boy in the trades of animal husbandry, farming, and weaponry making. An example of a son being trained in the family business is in today's Bible passage (2 Kings 4:18).

Were children taught to read? Among the wealthy—most likely just the men and boys—literacy seems more common. And in Judges, we have an example of someone reading—Gideon (Judges 8:13–14). But for most families, it's questionable whether reading and writing were part of the curriculum. Oral tradition, however, seems the most popular method of teaching lessons. The Torah instructed parents to have daily conversations with their kids about God's ways—whether hanging out at home, taking family walks, or putting the kids to bed (see Deuteronomy 6:7).

As modeled in this verse, the heart behind a child's education in ancient Israel was to free him or her to know, love, and follow God.

ENGAGE

The prophet Elisha asked the Shunammite woman, "What can we do for you?" (2 Kings 4:13), a question leading to God blessing the Shunammite woman with her heart's desire! Jesus asked similar questions—"What do you want me to do for you?" (Mark 10:51) or "What do you want?" (John 1:38)—before miraculously healing people or inviting them into His ministry. If Jesus were to ask you, "What can I do for you?" or "What do you want?" what would you tell Him?

Servant Girl of Naaman

2 KINGS 5:1–5, 9–15

The king of Aram had great admiration for Naaman, the commander of his army, because through him the LORD had given Aram great victories. But though Naaman was a mighty warrior, he suffered from **leprosy**.

At this time Aramean raiders had invaded the land of Israel, and among their captives was a young girl who had been given to Naaman's wife as a maid. One day the girl said to her mistress, "I wish my master would go to see the prophet in Samaria. He would heal him of his leprosy."

Or *a contagious skin disease*. The Hebrew word used throughout this passage—*tsara'ath*—can describe various skin diseases; see today's word study.

So Naaman told the king what the young girl from Israel had said. "Go and visit the prophet," the king of Aram told him. "I will send a letter of introduction for you to take to the king of Israel." So Naaman started out, carrying as gifts 750 pounds of silver, 150 pounds of gold, and ten sets of clothing.

. . . So Naaman went with his horses and chariots and waited at the door of Elisha's house. But Elisha sent a messenger out to him with this message: "Go and wash yourself seven times in the Jordan River. Then your skin will be restored, and you will be healed of your leprosy."

But Naaman became angry and stalked away. "I thought he would certainly come out to meet me!" he said. "I expected him to wave his hand over the leprosy and call on the name of the LORD his God and heal me! Aren't the rivers of Damascus, the Abana and the Pharpar, better than any of the rivers of Israel? Why shouldn't I wash in them and be healed?" So Naaman turned and went away in a rage.

But his officers tried to reason with him and said, "Sir, if the prophet had told you to do something very difficult, wouldn't you have done it? So you should certainly obey him when he says simply, 'Go and wash and be cured!'" So Naaman went down to the Jordan River and dipped himself seven times, as the man of God had instructed him. And his skin became as healthy as the skin of a young child, and he was healed!

Then Naaman and his entire party went back to find the man of God. They stood before him, and Naaman said, "Now I know that there is no God in all the world except in Israel. So please accept a gift from your servant."

A YOUNG GIRL'S FAITH

**If only my master would see the prophet who is in Samaria!
He would cure him of his leprosy.**

2 KINGS 5:3 NIV

Kayla, a young woman with a compassionate heart, was drawn to another country to help refugee children. Soon after, she was taken hostage, held for several years, tortured, and mistreated. Yet despite her circumstances, she put the welfare of other younger female captives above her own, enabling them to escape at the cost of her life. Courageous to the end, she even defended her faith in Jesus to her executioner.

In the book of 2 Kings, we see the story of another young captive. An unnamed Israelite girl was snatched by bandits from the neighboring region of Aram. There she became the servant of an army commander's wife; and there, despite potential harm, her compassion compelled her to show concern for her captors.

Her master, a soldier who valiantly served the king of Aram, suffered from the debilitating disease of leprosy (2 Kings 5:1–2). Despite her captivity, this girl cared enough to urge her mistress: "If only my master would see the prophet who is in Samaria! He would cure him of his leprosy" (v. 3 NIV). The wife told Naaman, and Naaman gained the king's permission to go. Soon Naaman left to seek the help of the prophet Elisha. There Naaman was healed and trusted in God (vv. 9–15)—all because he heeded the words of his young servant!

No matter the difficult situation we may face, God can empower us to reach out in faith, courage, and compassion to help others.

—Alyson Kieda

Is God calling you to share the love of Christ with someone? Talk to God about it, listening for His loving voice.

_____

_____

_____

_____

_____

_____

Identify a situation in your life causing you to feel confused, fearful, or anxious. Ask God for what you need to face that situation.

_____

_____

_____

_____

_____

_____

_____

Word Study

LEPROSY [NLT footnote—*a contagious skin disease*]

tsara'ath (2 Kings 5:3)

Mistranslated *leprosy*, Naaman's illness (*tsara'ath*) means "a contagious skin disease." In Leviticus, *tsara'ath* is an umbrella term to describe skin disorders ranging from psoriasis and eczema to ringworm (13–14). The description of bone disfigurement that characterizes modern leprosy isn't part of this list. Leprosy (Hansen's disease) wasn't widely recognized until the era of Alexander the Great.

Skin diseases carried stigmas. If you had a skin disorder in ancient Israel, you were ritually unclean (Leviticus 13–14). You had to quarantine (13:45–46). And you may have been seen as cursed (2 Kings 15:5). Throughout the Near East, skin diseases were feared. A Babylonian text reads: "If the skin of a man exhibits white *pusu*-areas or is dotted with *nuqdu* dots, such a man has been rejected by his god and is to be rejected by mankind."*

Though a man of integrity, the commander Naaman was probably an outcast, seen as cursed by the gods and rejected by his peers because of his skin disorder.

---

*John H. Walton, "2 Kings 5:1: *Leprosy*," in *NIV Cultural Backgrounds Study Bible* (Grand Rapids: Zondervan, 2016), 624.

ENGAGE

Compelled by compassion, the servant girl of Naaman helped him even though their nations were enemies. In Matthew 5, Jesus calls us to "Love [our] enemies!" (v. 44). He then says, "Pray for those who persecute you!" (v. 44). Identify an enemy—whether in your own life or at a national or international level—and pray for them.

_____

_____

_____

_____

_____

_____

_____

_____

_____

_____

_____

Follow-up: Commit to praying for them every day this week.

DAY 22

Huldah

2 KINGS 22:11–20

When the king heard what was written in the Book of the Law, he tore his clothes in despair. Then he gave these orders to Hilkiah the priest, Ahikam son of Shaphan, Acbor son of Micaiah, Shaphan the court secretary, and Asaiah the king's personal adviser: "Go to the Temple and speak to the LORD for me and for the people and for all Judah. Inquire about the words written in this scroll that has been found. For the LORD's great anger is burning against us because our ancestors have not obeyed the words in this scroll. We have not been doing everything it says we must do."

So Hilkiah the priest, Ahikam, Acbor, Shaphan, and Asaiah went to the New Quarter of Jerusalem to consult with the prophet Huldah. She was the wife of Shallum son of Tikvah, son of Harhas, the keeper of the Temple wardrobe.

She said to them, "The LORD, the God of Israel, has spoken! Go back and tell the man who sent you, 'This is what the LORD says: I am going to bring disaster on this city and its people. All the words written in the scroll that the king of Judah has read will come true. For my people have abandoned me and offered sacrifices to pagan gods, and I am very angry with them for everything they have done. My anger will burn against this place, and it will not be quenched.'

"But go to the king of Judah who sent you to seek the LORD and tell him: 'This is what the LORD, the God of Israel, says concerning the message you have just heard: You were sorry and humbled yourself before the LORD when you heard what I said against this city and its people—that this land would be cursed and become desolate. You tore your clothing in despair and wept before me in repentance. And I have indeed heard you, says the LORD. So I will not send the promised disaster until after you have died and been buried in peace. You will not see the disaster I am going to bring on this city.'"

So they took her message back to the king.

SETTING THE TRAJECTORY

Speak to the LORD for me and for the people and for all Judah. Inquire about the words written in this scroll that has been found.

2 KINGS 22:13

Mathematician Katherine Johnson played a pivotal role in a decisive moment in American history. In 1962, when NASA planned America's first orbit of the earth, astronaut John Glenn was skeptical of the new electronic calculating machines that plotted his trajectory. Before he would take flight, John sought Katherine's wisdom, asking her to perform the orbital calculations. She had conducted the trajectory analysis for America's first human space flight the year before—*by hand.* Only once she'd done the enormously complex manual calculations herself did he agree to go.

The wisdom of a woman named Huldah played a similarly vital role in the life of Judah. When God's law was rediscovered during temple renovations, Judah's young king Josiah "tore his robes" in grief because they'd not been following God's instructions (2 Kings 22:11 NIV). Before taking any action, Josiah "inquire[d] of the LORD" and sought advice from the prophet Huldah (v. 13 NIV).

Huldah explained that because the people had "forsaken [God] and burned incense to other gods and aroused [His] anger," disaster was coming (v. 17 NIV). But because Josiah's "heart was responsive" and he humbled himself before God (v. 19 NIV), the kingdom would have peace during his lifetime. Huldah's words helped initiate the kingdom's return to God.

May the skills and insights God bestows on us be used to benefit the lives of those around us. The godly influence we offer to even a single person might just ripple out to affect others, sometimes altering the trajectory of an entire nation.

—Kirsten Holmberg

PROFILE: HULDAH

A contemporary of the prophets Jeremiah and Zephaniah, Huldah appears to be a prominent, well-respected prophet. For after the discovery of the "Book of the Law" (2 Kings 22:8)—most likely a form of Deuteronomy— King Josiah's royal committee (v. 12) immediately turns to her for God's guidance (vv. 13–14). No one questions the authority of her prophetic response (v. 20).

The law's discovery happened at a pivotal time in the history of God's people. After King Solomon's reign, the kingdom had divided into the Northern Kingdom (Israel) and the Southern Kingdom (Judah). When God's law was rediscovered during Josiah's reign, the Northern Kingdom, Israel, had already been exiled by Assyria in 722 BC (2 Kings 17:5–7). The Southern Kingdom's exile by Babylon (586 BC) has not yet happened but seems inevitable (v. 16; 23:16–27). We can only imagine Josiah's devastation when he heard in the discovered book the many dire consequences for not following God's law—famine, disease, military defeat, and exile (Deuteronomy 28:15–68).

Huldah addressed Josiah's fears honestly. Her prophecy brings together two significant themes in 1 and 2 Kings—the unavoidable consequences of disobedience to God's law (2 Kings 22:16–17) as well as the ways God continues to show mercy to His repentant people, often by delaying judgment (vv. 19–20).

Describe a woman you know who is like Huldah, someone using her God-given wisdom, passions, and gifts to impact those around her.

_____

_____

_____

_____

_____

_____

How might God be inviting you to use your talents, gifts, and passions to extend His kingdom?

_____

_____

_____

_____

_____

_____

_____

_____

ENGAGE

Huldah tells Josiah that because he humbled himself before God and repented, he would experience security and peace. God still calls us to humble ourselves before Him in repentance and prayer. In Luke 18:13, Jesus shares a simple way to cry out to our loving heavenly Father: "God, have mercy on me, a sinner" (NIV). Today, this is known as the Jesus Prayer. Take two minutes to pray the Jesus Prayer, choosing one of its variations here:

Lord Jesus Christ, have mercy on me, a sinner.
Jesus, have mercy on me.
Jesus, have mercy.

As you repeat the prayer, let the words soak deeply into your heart. After the two minutes are up, journal about your prayer time. What was your experience of God as you prayed?*

---

*Adapted from Teresa A. Blythe, *50 Ways to Pray: Practices from Many Traditions and Times* (Nashville: Abingdon, 2006), 38–39.

DAY 23

Esther

ESTHER 4:13–17

Mordecai sent this reply to Esther: "Don't think for a moment that because you're in the palace you will escape when all other Jews are killed. If you keep quiet at a time like this, deliverance and relief for the Jews will arise from some other place, but you and your relatives will die. Who knows if perhaps you were made queen for just such a time as this?"

Then Esther sent this reply to Mordecai: "Go and gather together all the Jews of Susa and fast for me. Do not eat or drink for three days, night or day. My maids and I will do the same. And then, though it is against the law, I will go in to see the king. If I must die, I must die." So Mordecai went away and did everything as Esther had ordered him.

RIGHTEOUS AMONG THE NATIONS

Who knows if perhaps you were made queen for just such a time as this?

ESTHER 4:14

At Yad Vashem, the Holocaust museum in Israel, my husband and I went to the Garden of the Righteous Among the Nations that honors the men and women who risked their lives to save Jewish people during the Holocaust. While looking at the memorial, we met a group from the Netherlands. One woman was there to see her grandparents' names listed on the large plaques. Intrigued, we asked about her family's story.

Members of a resistance network, the woman's grandparents Reverend Pieter and Adriana Müller took in a two-year-old Jewish boy and passed him off as the youngest of their eight children from 1943 to 1945.

Moved by the story, we asked, "Did the little boy survive?" An older gentleman in the group stepped forward and proclaimed, "I am that boy!"

The bravery of many to act on behalf of the Jewish people reminds me of Queen Esther. The queen may have thought she could escape King Xerxes's decree to annihilate the Jews around 475 BC because she had concealed her ethnicity. However, she was convinced to act—even under the threat of death—when her cousin begged her not to remain silent about her Jewish heritage because she had been placed in her position "for just such a time as this" (Esther 4:14).

We may never be asked to make such a dramatic decision. However, we will likely face the choice to speak out against an injustice or remain silent; to provide assistance to someone in trouble or turn away. May God grant us courage.

—Lisa M. Samra

"Who knows if perhaps you were made . . . for just such a time as this?"

ESTHER 4:14

Are there people you need to speak up for? Ask God about the timing.

_____

_____

_____

_____

_____

_____

Identify when God gave you the courage to do the right thing.

_____

_____

_____

_____

_____

_____

_____

PROMISE IN EXILE

To many of the Jewish people in exile, God seemed silent.

Yet He was still working, largely behind the scenes. We see evidence of this in the book of Esther: Esther's extraordinary rise to power and her courageous role in the deliverance of God's people were clearly God's doing! Yet God's intervention was discreet—hidden. In fact, the book never mentions God's name at all! (Or *prayer* for that matter.) Yet God's plans for His people were unfolding, even during the period of waiting: the Jews gained special favor with Cyrus the Great, who helped them return to Israel (Ezra 1:1–4).

And God's greatest promise of all was being declared (Jeremiah 31:31–33; Ezekiel 16:59–63): God was initiating a new covenant with His people, to be fulfilled in Jesus. During the years of exile and waiting, God was readying the hearts of His people for the coming of His Son.

ENGAGE

Read Esther 4:13–17 again, identifying a word or phrase in Esther and Mordecai's dialogue that intrigues you. "Gaze" at your selected Scripture, as you might examine a shell, fossil, or pebble picked up at the beach.

What stands out to you as you allow its radiance, brilliant textures, and richness of meaning to emerge?

_____

_____

_____

_____

_____

_____

_____

_____

_____

_____

_____

_____

PART 2

Women
of the
New Testament

DAY 24

Elizabeth

LUKE 1:5–7, 24–25

When Herod was king of Judea, there was a Jewish priest named Zechariah. He was a member of the priestly order of Abijah, and his wife, Elizabeth, was also from the priestly line of Aaron. Zechariah and Elizabeth were righteous in God's eyes, careful to obey all of the Lord's commandments and regulations. They had no children because Elizabeth was unable to conceive, and they were both very old. . . .

Soon [after Gabriel visited Zechariah] his wife, Elizabeth, became pregnant and went into seclusion for five months. "How kind the Lord is!" she exclaimed. "He has taken away my disgrace of having no children."

FROM SHAME TO HONOR

"How kind the Lord is!" she exclaimed. "He has taken away
my disgrace of having no children."

Weddings, baby showers, and gender reveal parties give families the chance to celebrate the joys of new relationships and new life. Some of us, however, dread meeting certain "concerned" relatives at these gatherings whose questions can make those who are still single or child-less feel that there's something wrong with them.

Imagine the plight of Elizabeth, who was childless despite being mar-ried for many years. In her culture, that was seen as a sign of God's dis-favor (see 1 Samuel 1:5–6) and could actually be considered shameful. So while Elizabeth had been living righteously (Luke 1:6), her neighbors and relatives may have suspected otherwise.

Nonetheless, Elizabeth and her husband continued to serve the Lord faithfully. Then, when both were well advanced in years, a miracle occurred. God heard her prayer (Luke 1:13). He loves to show us His favor (v. 25). And though He may seem to delay, His timing is always right and His wisdom always perfect. For Elizabeth and her husband, God had a special gift: a child who would become the Messiah's fore-runner (Isaiah 40:3–5).

Do you feel inadequate because you seem to lack something—a uni-versity degree, a spouse, a child, a job, a house? Keep living for Him faithfully and waiting patiently for Him and His plan, just as Elizabeth did. No matter our circumstances, God is working in and through us. He knows your heart. He hears your prayers.

—Poh Fang Chia

Identify a prayer that has been answered, and thank God for His provision.

_____

_____

_____

_____

_____

_____

Talk to God about a prayer that is unanswered.

_____

_____

_____

_____

_____

_____

PROFILE: ELIZABETH

Luke has sometimes been called the "women's evangelist" because of how central women are in his presentation of the gospel story. In Luke 1, Elizabeth stands out as an example of faith, living with integrity and dignity (v. 6) in a culture where stigma against women without children was greater than we can imagine today. So great was the pressure for women to have children at that time that, in many Judean communities, if a woman did not have children for many years, the husband was urged to divorce her to have children with a different wife.

But Scripture tells another story about barren women, one where those once unable to have children are given significant roles in God's redemption story—Rebekah (Genesis 25:21), Rachel (Genesis 29:31; 30:22), Samson's mother (Judges 13:3), and Hannah (1 Samuel 1:5, 19–20). Elizabeth stands in that tradition, and responds to her experience of God's goodness and power with grateful wonder (Luke 1:25).

"Filled with the Holy Spirit" (v. 41)—a phrase that in Scripture indicates prophetic speech—Elizabeth is the first in Luke's gospel to confess that Jesus is "Lord" (v. 43).

ENGAGE

Talk to God about your deepest desire.

_____

_____

_____

_____

_____

DAY 25

Mary

LUKE 1:26–38

In the sixth month of Elizabeth's pregnancy, God sent the angel Gabriel to Nazareth, a village in Galilee, to a virgin named Mary. She was engaged to be married to a man named Joseph, a descendant of King David. Gabriel appeared to her and said, "Greetings, favored woman! The Lord is with you!"

Confused and disturbed, Mary tried to think what the angel could mean. "Don't be afraid, Mary," the angel told her, "for you have found **favor** with God! You will conceive and give birth to a son, and you will name him Jesus. He will be very great | Greek *charis*; see today's word study.

and will be called the Son of the Most High. The Lord God will give him the throne of his ancestor David. And he will reign over Israel forever; his Kingdom will never end!"

Mary asked the angel, "But how can this happen? I am a virgin."

The angel replied, "The Holy Spirit will come upon you, and the power of the Most High will overshadow you. So the baby to be born will be holy, and he will be called the Son of God. What's more, your relative Elizabeth has become pregnant in her old age! People used to say she was barren, but she has conceived a son and is now in her sixth month. For the word of God will never fail."

Mary responded, "I am the Lord's servant. May everything you have said about me come true." And then the angel left her.

A STRING OF YESES

Mary responded, "I am the Lord's servant. May everything you have said about me come true."

LUKE 1:38

My grandmother gave me a beautiful pearl necklace. The beautiful beads glowed about my neck until one day the string broke. Balls bounced in all directions off our home's hardwood flooring. Crawling over the planks, I recovered each tiny orb. On their own, they were small. But oh, when strung together, those pearls made such an impression!

Sometimes my yeses to God seem so insignificant—like those individual pearls. I compare myself with Mary, the mother of Jesus who was so fantastically obedient. She said yes when she embraced God's call for her to carry the Messiah. "I am the Lord's servant," Mary answered. "May everything you have said about me come true" (Luke 1:38). Did she understand all that would be required of her? That an even bigger yes to relinquishing her Son on the cross loomed ahead?

After the visits of the angels and shepherds, Luke 2:19 tells us that Mary "treasured up all these things and pondered them in her heart" (NIV). Treasure means to "store up." Ponder means to "thread together." The phrase is repeated of Mary in Luke 2:51. She would respond with many yeses over her lifetime.

As with Mary, the key to our obedience might be a threading together of various yeses to our Father's invitations, one at a time, until they string into the treasure of a surrendered life.

—**Elisa Morgan**

Identify a few yeses you've said to God during your life.
Talk to God about them.

_____

_____

_____

_____

_____

How do you feel drawn to say yes in this season? Ask God about it.

_____

_____

_____

_____

_____

_____

_____

Word Study

FAVOR

charis (Luke 1:30)

A significant word in Luke's gospel (not found in Matthew or Mark) is the Greek word *charis*—"favor" or "grace." Luke first uses a form of this word when Gabriel greets Mary as a "favored woman" (1:28). As a young female villager from Galilee (an area often looked down on by Judeans—see, for example, John 7:52), Mary would have had little social standing or power. So this respectful greeting surprises Mary (Luke 1:29–30). Mary's story echoes those of others in Scripture who found God's favor before being called to great tasks—Noah (Genesis 6:8) and Moses (Exodus 33:12–13).

As Mary celebrates in her song (Luke 1:46–55), God's favor shown to her while a "lowly servant girl" (v. 48) points beyond her to the hopes of Israel (v. 54) and all humanity. Through Jesus—who spoke with and embodied grace (4:22)—the world would experience a new era of God's gracious favor, a time in which social hierarchies would be turned upside down (1:52) so that all could experience God's goodness.

ENGAGE

Read Luke 1:26–38 a second time. What part of the dialogue between Mary and the angel Gabriel "comes alive" for you? Sit with that word, phrase, or sentence, inviting God into a conversation.

_____

_____

_____

Mary

LUKE 1:39–55

A few days later Mary hurried to the hill country of Judea, to the town where Zechariah lived. She entered the house and greeted Elizabeth. At the sound of Mary's greeting, Elizabeth's child leaped within her, and Elizabeth was filled with the Holy Spirit.

Elizabeth gave a glad cry and exclaimed to Mary, "God has blessed you above all women, and your child is blessed. Why am I so honored, that the mother of my Lord should visit me? When I heard your greeting, the baby in my womb jumped for joy. You are blessed because you believed that the Lord would do what he said."

Mary responded,

"Oh, how my soul praises the Lord.
  How my spirit rejoices in God my Savior!
For he took notice of his **lowly** servant girl,
  and from now on all generations will call me blessed.
For the Mighty One is holy,
  and he has done great things for me.
He shows mercy from generation to generation
    to all who fear him.
His mighty arm has done tremendous things!
  He has scattered the proud and haughty ones.
He has brought down princes from their thrones
    and exalted the humble.
He has filled the hungry with good things
  and sent the rich away with empty hands.
He has helped his servant Israel
  and remembered to be merciful.
For he made this promise to our ancestors,
    to Abraham and his children forever."

Greek *tapeinósis*; see today's biblical insight: Women behind the Magnificat.

153

MOSAIC OF PRAISE

Oh, how my soul praises the Lord. How my spirit rejoices in God my Savior!

LUKE 1:46–47

Sitting in the courtyard of the Church of the Visitation in Ein Karem, Israel, I was overwhelmed with the beautiful display of sixty-seven mosaics containing the words of Luke 1:46–55 in as many languages. Traditionally known as the Magnificat from the Latin "to magnify," these verses are Mary's joyous response to the announcement that she will be the mother of the Messiah.

Each plaque contains Mary's words, including: "Oh, how my soul praises the Lord. How my spirit rejoices in God my Savior! . . . For the Mighty One is holy, and he has done great things for me (vv. 46–47, 49). The biblical hymn etched in the tiles is a song of praise as Mary recounts the faithfulness of God to her and the nation of Israel.

A grateful recipient of God's grace, Mary rejoices in her salvation (v. 47). She acknowledges that God's mercy has extended to the Israelites for generations (v. 50). Looking back over God's care for the Israelites, Mary praises God for His powerful acts on behalf of His people (v. 51). She also thanks God, recognizing that her daily provision comes from His hand (v. 53).

Mary shows us that recounting the great things God has done for us is a way to express praise and can lead us to rejoice. Consider God's goodness today. In doing so, you may create a mosaic of great beauty with your words of praise.

—Lisa M. Samra

Identify one or two lines in Mary's Magnificat (Luke 1:46–55) that spark your interest. Reflect on what makes these verses meaningful or intriguing to you.

WOMEN BEHIND THE MAGNIFICAT

The Magnificat is a song of praise. While the words are Mary's (Luke 1:46), the Magnificat is a shared anthem.* It's the song of a sacred meeting (1:39–40) between two women, who—after almost certainly being stigmatized or shamed (v. 25)—experienced God's divine favor.

Mary and Elizabeth each suffered disgrace: Elizabeth was childless in a culture where a woman's worth centered on having children (v. 25). And Mary labeled herself "lowly" (v. 48), a word usually equated with poverty, low status, and marginalization. But God erased their humiliation: giving Elizabeth a son (vv. 24–25), and elevating the lowborn Mary to a status higher than any other woman (v. 42).

In its triumphant worship, the Magnificat captures the indescribable joy of Mary and Elizabeth in response to God's intervention in their lives. Meeting together for the first time since their change of fortunes (vv. 1:39–40), they are exultant, each in turn bursting forth in praise for the removal of their shame. First Elizabeth proclaims the coming Savior (v. 43). And, in response, Mary declares God's divine reversal—for Mary, for Elizabeth, and for anyone among God's people who felt unseen, ashamed, and invisible (vv. 50–53).

The One on the side of the oppressed had broken through!

---

*Some early manuscripts of Luke attribute the song to Elizabeth but more credit it to Mary.

ENGAGE

Make a list of the ways God has blessed you this year, taking time to thank Him for each one.

- _____
- _____
- _____
- _____
- _____
- _____
- _____
- _____
- _____
- _____
- _____
- _____
- _____
- _____
- _____

DAY 27

Anna

LUKE 2:36–38

Anna, a prophet, was also there in the Temple. She was the daughter of Phanuel from the tribe of Asher, and she was very old. Her husband died when they had been married only seven years. Then she lived as a widow to the age of **eighty-four**. She never left the Temple but stayed there day and night, worshiping God with fasting and prayer. She came along just as Simeon was talking with Mary and Joseph, and she began praising God. She talked about the child to everyone who had been waiting expectantly for God to rescue Jerusalem.

Anna may have been even older than eighty-four; NLT's alternative rendering of the verse is "[Anna] had been a widow for eighty-four years."

SEEING THE CHRIST

At that very moment, she gave thanks to God.

LUKE 2:38 NIV

Her eyesight might have been weak. At age eighty-four, Anna the prophet had lived in the temple in Jerusalem since she was widowed after just seven years of marriage—worshipping "night and day, fasting and praying" (Luke 2:37 NIV). Now, after all that time, she saw two young parents enter the temple carrying their infant son, and Anna's eyesight suddenly was never sharper.

The child was the Christ—yes, the Messiah—and Anna's spiritual eyes looked on with excitement to finally see the holy child. Finally, after years of waiting along with all of Israel for the promised Messiah. Neither uncertainty nor the hubbub around the child made her hesitate: "Coming up to them at that very moment, she gave thanks to God" (v. 38 NIV).

She then displayed a lesson for what modern believers are invited to do when we see God in our situations, especially after waiting, sometimes for years, for the Lord to show up with help and grace. Tell somebody about Him. Witness and testify. In doing so, we follow in the way of the prophet Anna, who "spoke about the child to all who were looking forward to the redemption of Jerusalem" (v. 38 NIV).

Her witness confirmed who He was. But her testimony also declared what He can do—redeem. Faithfully waiting on God is a way of life that, if followed, helps us finally see—His answers, our blessings, and His arrival.

—Patricia Raybon

159

What does Anna teach us about what to do while waiting on God?

_____

_____

_____

_____

_____

_____

What can we learn from her story about looking for God and His help,
rather than focusing on worries or problems?

_____

_____

_____

_____

_____

_____

_____

_____

WOMEN AS WITNESSES

Elizabeth, Mary, and Anna were among the first to proclaim that Christ was the Messiah. Throughout the Gospels, we see women testify to Christ's identity and bear witness to His birth, death, and resurrection. In fact, one of the reasons that the gospel accounts of the death and resurrection of Jesus are seen as credible is *because* women were recorded as witnesses.

During the time of Jesus, rabbis debated whether or not women's testimonies could even qualify for the minimum number of witnesses required for a case (Deuteronomy 19:15).* Although there were times when women testified in court, evidence shows it was avoided if possible. The first-century Jewish historian Josephus said that women were disqualified because of "giddiness and impetuosity."† So if Jesus's resurrection was made up by some of His followers, it's highly unlikely they would have consistently described women as the first witnesses to these claims.

The gospel accounts of Jesus's resurrection don't read like an invention but rather as the testimony of those who'd encountered an event they found nearly impossible to believe (Luke 24:11)—the resurrection of one person, through whom reality itself had changed. As New Testament scholar N. T. Wright puts it: "The gospel is good news not least because it dares to tell us things we didn't expect, weren't inclined to believe, and couldn't understand." Through Jesus's resurrection, God's future had broken into the present reality, lifting up women and men alike to be a part of that good future.

God gave women the tremendous privilege of being the first to proclaim the birth of the Savior and to encounter the resurrected Jesus (Matthew 28:1–18; Luke 24:1–11; John 20:11–18)—because God has always valued and included women in the redemption story.

---

*"Women as Witnesses," in *The IVP Women's Bible Commentary*, ed. Catherine Clark Kroeger and Mary J. Evans (Downers Grove: InterVarsity Press, 2002), 560–61.

†Tal Ilan, *Jewish Women in Greco-Roman Palestine* (Peabody, MA: Hendrickson, 1996), 163–66, in Joel B. Green, *The Gospel of Luke: The New International Commentary on the New Testament* (Grand Rapids, MI: Eerdmans, 1997), 839–840.

ENGAGE

Anna was sensitive to God's presence. Identify activities, environments, or times when you more easily see God at work or feel closest to Him.

_____

_____

_____

_____

_____

_____

_____

_____

_____

_____

_____

_____

Thank You, Jesus, for the gift of Your presence. I love seeing Your fingerprints in the commonplace, everyday moments and in the extraordinary. May I grow in trusting You are at work in every area of my life. In the power of Your name, amen.

Faithfully waiting on God is a way of life that, if followed, helps us finally see—His answers, our blessings, and His arrival.

DAY 28

Samaritan Woman

JOHN 4:6–10, 15–19, 25–30, 39

Jesus, tired from the long walk, sat wearily beside the well about noontime. Soon a Samaritan woman came to draw water, and Jesus said to her, "Please give me a drink." He was alone at the time because his disciples had gone into the village to buy some food.

The woman was surprised, for Jews refuse to have anything to do with Samaritans. She said to Jesus, "You are a Jew, and I am a Samaritan woman. Why are you asking me for a drink?"

Jesus replied, "If you only knew the gift God has for you and who you are speaking to, you would ask me, and I would give you living water." . . .

"Please, sir," the woman said, "give me this water! Then I'll never be thirsty again, and I won't have to come here to get water."

"Go and get your husband," Jesus told her.

"I don't have a husband," the woman replied.

Jesus said, "You're right! You don't have a husband—for you have had five husbands, and you aren't even married to the man you're living with now. You certainly spoke the truth!"

"Sir," the woman said, "you must be a prophet. . . . I know the Messiah is coming—the one who is called Christ. When he comes, he will explain everything to us."

Then Jesus told her, "I AM the Messiah!"

Just then his disciples came back. They were shocked to find him talking to a woman, but none of them had the nerve to ask, "What do you want with her?" or "Why are you talking to her?" The woman left her water jar beside the well and ran back to the village, telling everyone, "Come and see a man who told me everything I ever did! Could he possibly be the Messiah?" So the people came streaming from the village to see him. . . .

Many Samaritans from the village believed in Jesus because the woman had said, "He told me everything I ever did!"

BARRIERS AND BLESSINGS

Then Jesus told her, "I AM the Messiah!"

JOHN 4:26

What did Jesus see when He looked at the woman at the well in John 4? He saw someone who wanted acceptance and desperately needed to know she was loved. Most of all, He saw someone who needed what only He could give—a new heart.

It was no accident that the disciples had all gone to town to buy food. Surely, they would have tried to warn Jesus not to talk to this person—a woman, a Samaritan, and someone with a bad reputation.

Not being one to follow protocol, however, Jesus used this encounter to bless her with the truth of "living water" (v. 10). In just one conversation, He broke down barriers of old hostilities, of gender bias, of ethnic and racial divides. And this woman became the first of many Samaritans to confess that Jesus was the Messiah (vv. 39–42).

When she told others of her encounter with a Man who knew "everything I ever did" (v. 39), she was already practicing the planting and harvesting that Jesus was teaching His followers (John 4:35–38). Many believed that day, and later Philip, Peter, John, and others would preach in Samaria and lead many more to Christ (Acts 8:5–14; 15:3).

When we tell others of our own "encounter" with Jesus, we bless them with living water.

—**Cindy Hess Kasper**

How are you being invited to accept someone as Jesus
accepted the Samaritan woman?

_____

_____

_____

_____

_____

_____

Where in your life do you need hope, as the Samaritan woman did?
Talk to God about it.

_____

_____

_____

_____

_____

_____

PROFILE: SAMARITAN WOMAN

The story of Jesus's interaction with the unnamed Samaritan woman is a remarkable one in which Jesus calmly crosses gender, ethnic, and religious divides to reveal Himself to her and the Samaritan people.

It's easy for us to assume that a woman having had five marriages and currently living with a man not her husband (John 4:18) must have particularly poor moral character. But marriage was an economic necessity for most women in Jesus's day, and it was husbands, not wives, who typically had the legal right to divorce. This power disparity could easily be abused, an injustice Jesus confronts when criticizing husbands who divorced for frivolous reasons (Matthew 5:31–32). So the Samaritan woman likely found it necessary to remarry repeatedly, whether due to previous husbands' deaths or due to husbands divorcing her. It wouldn't have been any woman's preference to be with a man unwilling to give her the security of a marriage commitment, as seems to be her current situation.

Jesus's words revealed He knew and cared about this woman's story in its pain and desperation. His words do not offend her, but lead to her believing His claim to be the Messiah and becoming the first evangelist (John 4:29–30, 39–42).

JEWS AND SAMARITANS

Why did "Jews refuse to have anything to do with Samaritans" (John 4:9)? Samaritans saw Mount Gerizim, not Jerusalem, as the correct central place of worship (v. 20) and accepted only the first five books of Hebrew Scripture as authoritative. Samaritans saw themselves as living out the true form of Israelite faith, while first-century Jews often saw them as unorthodox semi-pagans.

ENGAGE

Which part of today's story found in John 4 stands out to you? Journal and reflect on that part, asking God what He might be inviting you to through the Scripture reading.

_____

_____

_____

_____

_____

_____

_____

_____

_____

_____

_____

_____

_____

_____

_____

DAY 29

Woman with the Issue of Blood

LUKE 8:43–48

A woman in the crowd had suffered for twelve years with constant bleeding, and she could find no cure. Coming up behind Jesus, she touched the fringe of his robe. Immediately, the bleeding stopped.

"Who touched me?" Jesus asked.

Everyone denied it, and Peter said, "Master, this whole crowd is pressing up against you."

But Jesus said, "Someone deliberately touched me, for I felt healing power go out from me." When the woman realized that she could not stay hidden, she began to tremble and fell to her knees in front of him. The whole crowd heard her explain why she had touched him and that she had been immediately healed. "Daughter," he said to her, "your faith has made you well. Go in peace."

NEVER GIVE UP HOPE

"Daughter," [Jesus] said to her, "your faith has made you well. Go in peace."

LUKE 8:48

When my friend received a diagnosis of cancer, the doctor advised her to get her affairs in order. She called me, sobbing, worried about her husband and young children. I shared her urgent prayer request with our mutual friends. We rejoiced when a second doctor encouraged her to never give up hope and confirmed his team would do all they could to help. Though some days were harder than others, she focused on God instead of the odds stacked against her. She never gave up.

My friend's persevering faith reminds me of the desperate woman in Luke 8. Weary from twelve years of ongoing suffering, disappointment, and isolation, she approached Jesus from behind and stretched her hand toward the hem of His robe. Her immediate healing followed her act of faith: persistently hoping . . . believing Jesus was able to do what others couldn't . . . no matter how impossible her situation seemed (vv. 43–44).

We may experience pain that feels endless, situations that appear hopeless, or waiting that seems unbearable. We may endure moments when the odds against us are stacked high and wide. We may not experience the healing we long for as we continue trusting Christ. But even then, Jesus invites us to keep reaching for Him, to trust Him and never give up hope, and to believe He is always able, always trustworthy, and always within reach.

—Xochitl Dixon

How have you recently needed to trust in Jesus despite the challenges you faced? What hope have you found in Him?

_____

_____

_____

_____

_____

_____

Talk to God about an area of your life in which you need healing.

_____

_____

_____

_____

_____

_____

_____

_____

JESUS AND WOMEN

Throughout His public ministry, Jesus treated women respectfully. Jesus had meaningful extended conversations with women (John 4:3–27; 11:21–26), taught in a woman's home (Luke 10:38), and included women among his disciples (Matthew 12:48–50; Luke 8:1–3). He lifted up women as examples (Mark 12:41–44) and spoke against women's exploitation (Matthew 5:32). Jesus insisted that women have a place of dignity and significance in God's kingdom as His disciples and that this must not "be taken away from her" (Luke 10:42).

This is noteworthy because at the time of Jesus, Greek culture influenced Jewish life in Palestine. Many Greek philosophers, including Plato (437 to 347 BC) and Aristotle (384 to 322 BC), spoke of women as inferior. Legally, women in first-century Greek and Jewish culture were often treated as their husband's property. Most women lacked access to education. Some movements within the first century promoted higher status, rights, and new roles for women, however. Women's treatment, rights, and social power could vary greatly depending on what region they lived in.

Some first-century Jewish thinkers expressed beliefs similar to those found in Greek philosophy. The Jewish philosopher Philo (20 BC to AD 40), for example, wrote that "the woman, being imperfect and depraved by nature, made the beginning of sinning" while man, "the more excellent and perfect creature," was the first example of repentance and "indeed of every good feeling and action." But others, such as the highly revered teacher Gamaliel, who taught Paul (Acts 5:34; 22:3), spoke respectfully of women and treated men and women equally in his legal guidelines.

ENGAGE

Enter into today's story by imagining yourself as the woman with the issue of blood. Feel the intensity of your desire to be healed as you push your way through the crowd toward the Healer. When you reach Jesus, grab the fringe of His robe. How do you experience His healing? Look up and see the love in Jesus's eyes as He says, "Daughter . . . your faith has made you well. Go in peace" (Luke 8:48).

_____

_____

_____

_____

_____

How do you feel? What do you want to tell Him?

_____

_____

_____

_____

_____

_____

_____

Jesus invites us to keep reaching for Him, to trust Him and never give up hope.

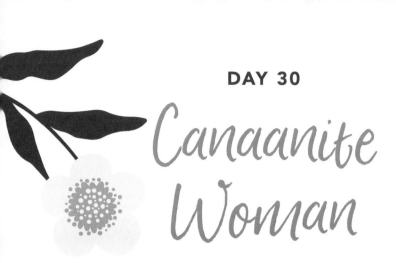

DAY 30

Canaanite Woman

MATTHEW 15:21–28

Then Jesus left Galilee and went north to the region of Tyre and Sidon. A **Gentile** woman who lived there came to him, pleading, "Have mercy on me, O Lord, Son of David! For my daughter is possessed by a demon that torments her severely."

Greek *Canaanite*.

But Jesus gave her no reply, not even a word. Then his disciples urged him to send her away. "Tell her to go away," they said. "She is bothering us with all her begging."

Then Jesus said to the woman, "I was sent only to help God's lost sheep—the people of Israel."

But she came and worshiped him, pleading again, "Lord, help me!"

Jesus responded, "It isn't right to take food from the children and throw it to the dogs."

She replied, "That's true, Lord, but even dogs are allowed to eat the scraps that fall beneath their masters' table."

"Dear woman," Jesus said to her, "your faith is great. Your request is granted." And her daughter was instantly healed.

EVEN WHEN HE IS SILENT

"Dear woman," Jesus said to her, **"your faith is great.
Your request is granted."**

MATTHEW 15:28

The mother was at her wits' end. She must have sought all available help and tried every method. But her daughter remained out of control. If she didn't find a solution soon, she might lose her daughter—forever.

Then she heard that a foreign healer had come to town. Hope sparked in her heart. She came to Jesus crying, "Have mercy on me! My daughter is demon-possessed and suffering terribly" (Matthew 15:22 NIV). But her heartfelt plea was met with what must have felt like cold silence (v. 23), and His disciples tried to send her away. So, she flung herself at Jesus's feet, pleading, "Lord, help me!" (v. 25). Jesus replied that it wouldn't be right to take the children's bread and toss it to the household pet dog.

These words may sound harsh, but the woman caught a glimmer of hope. She realized that though she wasn't a child in the family eligible for the choicest food, she could receive what might fall from the master's table. So, she humbly asked for a crumb. Jesus rewarded her faith by healing her daughter at that moment (v. 28).

Whatever the need in our life may be today, we could take a lesson from this woman: Get that need to Jesus! God's silence is not an indication of His unwillingness to meet our need. Sometimes He's stretching our faith, drawing it out—as He does with this Canaanite woman.

—Poh Fang Chia

Identify an area in your life where your faith is being stretched.

_____

_____

_____

_____

_____

_____

Tell God how you've experienced being stretched in your faith.
How does God respond to you?

_____

_____

_____

_____

_____

_____

_____

_____

_____

PROFILE: CANAANITE WOMAN

Scripture is filled with examples of persistence with God—even arguing and debating with God (like Jacob, Genesis 32:26)—being rewarded. In Jesus's time, rabbis would test prospective disciples' persistence, sometimes turning a prospective disciple away several times or presenting them with another obstacle before their persistence proved their commitment.

The unnamed Canaanite woman in Matthew 15:22–28 is a remarkable example of the kind of persistent faith God rewards. Jesus initially doesn't respond to her plea (v. 23). When Jesus does speak with her, He explains His primary calling at this point is to God's chosen people, Israel (v. 24; 10:5–6). When the woman still persists in pleading (15:25), Jesus responds with a cryptic metaphor about not feeding table food to the dogs.

The metaphor Jesus uses is one from the woman's context—while gentiles sometimes kept dogs as pets, Jews never would. Jewish people saw dogs as pests and vermin, and "dog" could even be a term of insult for gentiles. But in the original Greek, we can see that Jesus chooses the word for "little dogs" or puppies.

The woman rises to the occasion with brilliant quick wit, suggesting that if Israel really is God's chosen people, then gentiles too were meant to be blessed by them (v. 27). Someone the disciples wanted to dismiss as merely a nuisance (v. 23) is instead lifted up by Jesus as a role model of persistent faith (v. 28).

God's silence is not
an indication of His
unwillingness to
meet our need.

ENGAGE

What word, phrase, or image from Matthew 15:21–28 stands out to you? Reflect on that part of the passage, asking God, What truths do I need to hear today through this part of the story? Journal His response.

Woman Caught in Adultery

JOHN 8:1–11

Jesus returned to the Mount of Olives, but early the next morning he was back again at the Temple. A crowd soon gathered, and he sat down and taught them. As he was speaking, the teachers of religious law and the Pharisees brought a woman who had been caught in the act of adultery. They put her in front of the crowd.

"Teacher," they said to Jesus, "this woman was caught in the act of adultery. The law of Moses says to stone her. What do you say?"

They were trying to trap him into saying something they could use against him, but Jesus stooped down and wrote in the dust with his finger. They kept demanding an answer, so he stood up again and said, "All right, but let the one who has never sinned throw the first stone!" Then he stooped down again and wrote in the dust.

When the accusers heard this, they slipped away one by one, beginning with the oldest, until only Jesus was left in the middle of the crowd with the woman. Then Jesus stood up again and said to the woman, "Where are your accusers? Didn't even one of them condemn you?"

"No, Lord," she said.

And Jesus said, "Neither do I. Go and sin no more."

FORGIVEN AND FREE

"Neither do I condemn you," said Jesus. "Go, and from now on do not sin anymore."

JOHN 8:11 CSB

I shared details from my *BJ Days* (Before Jesus) with a group of women. After confessing sins I'd once worn as a badge of honor, I said, "Then I heard the gospel. Jesus *started* changing my life."

One woman said, "Be careful. No one will invite you to speak at their church if they know those things about you."

Shame had my tongue on lockdown. Still, I longed to share God's redeeming truth and love with others. So, I searched the Bible for the key to *feeling* forgiven.

When religious leaders publicly shamed a woman caught in adultery, Jesus didn't condone her sins, chastise her, or demand she clean up her act before coming to Him. Rather, Jesus spoke to those who condemned her: "Let any one of you who is without sin be the first to throw a stone at her" (John 8:7 NIV).

"At this, those who heard began to go away one at a time, the older ones first, until only Jesus was left, with the woman still standing there" (v. 9 NIV).

"Neither do I condemn you," said Jesus. "Go, and *from now on* do not sin anymore" (v. 11 CSB).

No matter what happened in our *BJ Days* or how we fall short as we surrender to the life-transforming love of Christ daily, God offers mercy when we repent. Scars from our past become beautiful signs of redemption, as we believe we're forgiven and free to live for Jesus without condemnation.

—Xochitl Dixon

183

When have you felt weighed down by guilt and shame over past sins?

_____

_____

_____

_____

_____

_____

How has confessing your sins helped you move forward with confidence in Christ's gift of forgiveness?

_____

_____

_____

_____

_____

_____

_____

THE CASE AGAINST HER

We will never know her name. But one thing is clear: when she was dragged in front of the temple crowds (John 8:3), under Roman law she should've been protected. Only the governor could authorize executions. But the Pharisees were exploiting her to "trap" Jesus (v. 6): At Judaism's most sacred place, the temple—and in front of a large crowd of religious pilgrims—they were questioning Jesus's reputation as a holy man—a religious teacher. The crowd of devout Jews knew the Torah's punishment for an adulterer caught in the act—stoning (Leviticus 20:10). If Jesus went against the Torah, He would be seen as an unrighteous Jew. His ministry discredited. To order her execution, however, would be rebellion against Rome.

In His response, Jesus saved her life and averted a riot were the Roman troops to get involved. In the process, He also revealed Himself to be a true prophet—maintaining the spirit behind the Law in valuing human life. And He saw the woman as a person, not—as the Pharisees and the religious teachers did—as a tool to be exploited in front of a mob.

ENGAGE

In your imagination, visualize yourself standing face-to-face with Jesus. Hear Him say these words to you, "Neither do I condemn you" (John 8:11). Let those words soak into your mind and heart. What is it like to hear these words of freedom and forgiveness from Him? How do you respond to Him?

_____

_____

_____

_____

DAY 32

Martha of Bethany

LUKE 10:38–42

As Jesus and the disciples continued on their way to Jerusalem, they came to a certain village where a woman named Martha welcomed him into her home. Her sister, Mary, sat **at the Lord's feet**, listening to what he taught. But Martha was distracted by the big dinner she was preparing. She came to Jesus and said, "Lord, doesn't it seem unfair to you that my sister just sits here while I do all the work? Tell her to come and help me."

Greek *para iēsous pous*; see today's word study.

But the Lord said to her, "My dear Martha, you are worried and upset over all these details! There is only one thing worth being concerned about. Mary has discovered it, and it will not be taken away from her."

THE MAIN EVENT

There is only one thing worth being concerned about. Mary has discovered it, and it will not be taken away from her.

LUKE 10:42

While watching a fireworks display during a celebration in my city, I became distracted. Off to the right and the left of the main event, smaller fireworks occasionally popped up in the sky. They were good, but watching them caused me to miss parts of the more spectacular display directly above me.

Sometimes good things take us away from something better. That happened in the life of Martha, whose story is recorded in Luke 10:38–42. When Jesus and His disciples arrived in the village of Bethany, Martha welcomed them into her home. Being a good host meant that someone had to prepare the meal for the guests, so it's not surprising that Martha was busy with meal preparations.

When Martha complained that her sister Mary wasn't helping, Jesus defended Mary's choice to sit at His feet. But the Lord wasn't saying that Mary was more spiritual than her sister. Martha, too, is portrayed as a friend and follower of Jesus who had great faith (John 11:26–27). And He wasn't being critical of Martha's desire to look after their physical needs. Jesus Himself cared for people's physical needs. Rather, what the Lord wanted Martha to hear is that in the busyness of our service, listening to Him is the main event.

—Anne Cetas

187

Identify a distraction in your life right now. Talk to God about it.

_____

_____

_____

_____

_____

_____

Do you identify more with Martha's or Mary's personality? Why?

_____

_____

_____

_____

_____

_____

_____

Word Study

AT THE FEET [NLT translation—*at the Lord's feet*]

para iēsous pous (Luke 10:39)

It's easy for us today to miss the profound significance of the phrase "at the Lord's feet" (Luke 10:39). To sit at the teacher's feet was to identify publicly as the rabbi's disciple. It's the same phrase Paul uses to describe himself training under the highly respected rabbi Gamaliel ("at the feet of Gamaliel," Acts 22:3 NKJV). And in Jesus's day, only males were taught the Torah in rabbinic schools.

In this scene, Jesus is not scolding Martha for her faithful service—a quality central to Jesus's vision of servant leadership and discipleship (Luke 22:24–27). Instead, Jesus is warning Martha against the danger of worry in her own discipleship and service, a theme we see elsewhere in Luke (8:14; 12:22–32). And Jesus is uplifting the importance of Mary's decision to identify herself publicly as Jesus's disciple.

ENGAGE

Enter into today's Bible story as Martha or Mary. When Jesus arrives and begins teaching at your home, how do you feel about it? Where are you in the scene? Are you happy to be engaged in your current activity, or would you prefer to be doing something else? What do you want Jesus to know? Tell Him. How does He respond to you?

DAY 33

Sisters of Bethany

JOHN 11:21–36, 43–44

Martha said to Jesus, "Lord, if only you had been here, my brother would not have died. But even now I know that God will give you whatever you ask."

Jesus told her, "Your brother will rise again."

"Yes," Martha said, "he will rise when everyone else rises, at the last day."

Jesus told her, "I am the resurrection and the life. Anyone who believes in me will live, even after dying. Everyone who lives in me and believes in me will never ever die. Do you believe this, Martha?"

"Yes, Lord," she told him. "I have always believed you are the Messiah, the Son of God, the one who has come into the world from God." Then she returned to Mary. She called Mary aside from the mourners and told her, "The Teacher is here and wants to see you." So Mary immediately went to him.

Jesus had stayed outside the village, at the place where Martha met him. When the people who were at the house consoling Mary saw her leave so hastily, they assumed she was going to Lazarus's grave to weep. So they followed her there. When Mary arrived and saw Jesus, she fell at his feet and said, "Lord, if only you had been here, my brother would not have died."

When Jesus saw her weeping and saw the other people wailing with her, a deep anger welled up within him, and he was deeply troubled. "Where have you put him?" he asked them.

They told him, "Lord, come and see." Then Jesus wept. The people who were standing nearby said, "See how much he loved him!" . . .

Then Jesus shouted, "Lazarus, come out!" And the dead man came out, his hands and feet bound in graveclothes, his face wrapped in a headcloth. Jesus told them, "Unwrap him and let him go!"

DELAY MAY NOT MEAN DENIAL

**Jesus told her, "I am the resurrection and the life. . . .
Do you believe this, Martha?"**

JOHN 11:25–26

My sons' birthdays are in December. When they were small, Angus quickly learned that if he didn't receive a longed-for toy for his birthday at the beginning of the month, it might be in his Christmas stocking. And if David didn't receive his gift for Christmas, it might appear for his birthday four days later. Delay didn't necessarily mean denial.

It was natural for Martha and Mary to send for Jesus when Lazarus became seriously ill (John 11:1–3). Perhaps they looked anxiously along the road for signs of His arrival, but Jesus didn't come. The funeral service had been over for four days when Jesus finally walked into town (v. 17).

Martha was blunt. "If only you had been here," she said, "my brother would not have died" (v. 21). Then her faith flickered into certainty, "But even now I know that God will give you whatever you ask" (v. 22). I wonder what she expected. Lazarus was dead, and she was wary about opening the tomb. And yet at a word from Jesus, Lazarus's spirit returned to his decaying body (vv. 41–44). Jesus had bypassed simply healing His sick friend, in order to perform the far greater miracle of bringing him back to life.

Waiting for God's timing may also give us a greater miracle than we had hoped for.

—Marion Stroud

Do you have any hopes or dreams that need to be resurrected?
Talk to God about them.

_____

_____

_____

_____

_____

_____

_____

_____

_____

_____

_____

_____

_____

_____

_____

FIRST-CENTURY JEWISH BELIEFS ABOUT RESURRECTION OF THE DEAD

What did first-century Jewish people believe about the afterlife? One religious group, the Essenes, believed that only the soul, not the body, lived forever. Another group of religious teachers, the Pharisees, firmly believed in a future, bodily resurrection, while the Sadducees denied a future resurrection (Matthew 22:23; Acts 23:8). But it's likely that the majority of first-century Judean and Galilean Jews believed in a future, bodily resurrection.

We see this belief reflected in Martha's words that her brother would rise "when everyone else rises, at the last day" (John 11:24). Martha's words reflect a cherished hope for Jewish people—that the current age would be replaced by an entirely different future age and a transformed creation. In order for this promised future to be fair, it was believed, all those faithful to God who had already died—like Lazarus—would be resurrected at the very end of the current age ("at the last day") to join in that future age. In this way, evil would be defeated and God's justice would prevail.

Jesus's bodily resurrection—the resurrection of one person before this final mass resurrection—entirely transformed how early believers understood that future hope. As Jesus revealed to Martha, the hope of the resurrection and the future age was no longer only a distant hope, but a reality already accessible in Jesus (v. 25).

193

ENGAGE

In today's passage, Jesus told Martha the truth about Himself and then asked her, "Do you believe this, Martha?" (John 11:26). What truth about Jesus, the Bible, or the Christian faith makes you wonder, Do I believe this? Reflect on the doubts and questions you may have, and talk to Jesus about them.

Waiting for God's timing may give us a greater miracle than we had hoped for.

DAY 34

Mary of Bethany

JOHN 12:1–8

Six days before the Passover celebration began, Jesus arrived in Bethany, the home of Lazarus—the man he had raised from the dead. A dinner was prepared in Jesus' honor. Martha served, and Lazarus was among those who ate with him. Then Mary took a twelve-ounce jar of expensive perfume made from essence of nard, and she anointed Jesus' feet with it, wiping his feet with her hair. The house was filled with the fragrance.

But Judas Iscariot, the disciple who would soon betray him, said, "That perfume was worth a year's wages. It should have been sold and the money given to the poor." Not that he cared for the poor—he was a thief, and since he was in charge of the disciples' money, he often stole some for himself.

Jesus replied, "Leave her alone. She did this in preparation for my burial. You will always have the poor among you, but you will not always have me."

LET DOWN YOUR HAIR

Then Mary took a twelve-ounce jar of expensive perfume made from essence of nard, and she anointed Jesus' feet with it, wiping his feet with her hair.

JOHN 12:3

Shortly before Jesus was crucified, a woman named Mary poured a bottle of expensive perfume on His feet. Then, in what may have been an even more daring act, she wiped His feet with her hair (John 12:3). Not only did Mary sacrifice what may have been her life's savings, she also sacrificed her reputation. In first-century Middle Eastern culture, respectable women never let down their hair in public. But true worship is not concerned about what others think of us (2 Samuel 6:21–22). To worship Jesus, Mary was willing to be thought of as immodest, perhaps even immoral.

Some of us may feel pressured to be perfect when we go to church so that people will think well of us. Metaphorically speaking, we work hard to make sure we have every hair in place. But a healthy church is a place where we can let down our hair and not hide our flaws behind a façade of perfection. In church, we should be able to reveal our weaknesses to find strength rather than conceal our faults to appear strong.

Worship doesn't involve behaving as if nothing is wrong; it's making sure everything is right—right with God and with one another. When our greatest fear is letting down our hair, perhaps our greatest sin is keeping it up.

—Julie Ackerman Link

Identify an area of your life where you're being challenged to grow in vulnerability and courage.

_____

_____

_____

_____

_____

_____

In what ways has God helped you become more open and honest, even in your imperfections?

_____

_____

_____

_____

_____

_____

NARD

Pure nard or spikenard (Mark 14:3) is an aromatic oil from a plant root grown in the Himalayas. This explains its costliness—"a year's wages" (v. 5) or "more than three hundred denarii" (ESV). A denarius was a full day's wage for a laborer.

Because its fragrance is often associated with a bride on her wedding day (Song of Solomon 1:12; 4:13–14 ESV), some scholars believe Mary gave her most precious possession—her personal dowry—to Jesus. Mary's anointing of Jesus with the expensive nard was timely and necessary. When Jesus died, His body was hastily prepared for burial because of the Sabbath observance (Mark 15:42–46). A group of women had planned to go to the tomb to anoint His body after the Sabbath (16:1), but by that time Jesus had already risen. But six days earlier (John 12:1), Mary had anointed Jesus with perfume "to prepare for [His] burial" (Mark 14:8 NIV).

ENGAGE

Who grabs your attention in today's Bible passage? Is it Mary for her bold act of faith, Judas for his hypocrisy, or Jesus for coming to Mary's defense? In this exercise, have a conversation with him or her, trying to see the Scripture with fresh eyes.

Follow-up: What did you discover about this person, God, or yourself? Did anything come up that surprised you?

Women at the Cross

MARK 15:33–41

At noon, darkness fell across the whole land until three o'clock. Then at three o'clock Jesus called out with a loud voice, "Eloi, Eloi, lema sabachthani?" which means "My God, my God, why have you abandoned me?"

Some of the bystanders misunderstood and thought he was calling for the prophet Elijah. One of them ran and filled a sponge with sour wine, holding it up to him on a reed stick so he could drink. "Wait!" he said. "Let's see whether Elijah comes to take him down!"

Then Jesus uttered another loud cry and breathed his last. And the curtain in the sanctuary of the Temple was torn in two, from top to bottom.

When the Roman officer who stood facing him saw how he had died, he exclaimed, "This man truly was the Son of God!"

Some women were there, watching from a distance, including Mary Magdalene, Mary (the mother of James the younger and of Joseph), and Salome. They had been followers of Jesus and had cared for him while he was in Galilee. Many other women who had come with him to Jerusalem were also there.

STANDING FIRM

Stand firm. Let nothing move you.

1 CORINTHIANS 15:58 NIV

In the Middle Eastern country where they live, Adrian and his family suffer persecution for their faith. Yet, through it all, they demonstrate Christ's love. Standing in his church courtyard on Good Friday, which was pummeled by bullets when terrorists used it as training ground, he said, "Today is Good Friday. We remember that Jesus suffered for us on the cross." And suffering, he continued, is something that believers in Jesus there understand. But his family chooses to remain in their homeland: "We're still here, still standing."

These believers follow the example of the women who stood watching as Jesus died on the cross (Mark 15:40). They—including Mary Magdalene, Mary the mother of James and Joseph, and Salome—were brave to stay there, for friends and family members of an enemy of the state could be ridiculed and punished. Yet the women showed their love for Jesus by their very presence with Him. Even as they "followed him and cared for his needs" in Galilee (v. 41 NIV), they stood with Him at His hour of deepest need.

When we remember the greatest gift of our Savior—His death on a cross—take a moment to consider how we can stand for Jesus as we face trials of many kinds (see James 1:2–4). Think too about our fellow believers around the world who suffer for their faith. As Adrian asked, "Can you please stand with us in your prayers?"

—Amy Boucher Pye

What does standing for Christ look like in your neighborhood?

_____

_____

_____

_____

_____

_____

How can you support persecuted believers around the world?

_____

_____

_____

_____

_____

_____

_____

PROFILE: WOMEN AT THE CROSS

Who were the women who witnessed Jesus's crucifixion? Among the "many" women there, Mark lists three by name: Mary Magdalene, Mary the mother of James the younger and of Joseph, and Salome (Mark 15:40–41). Mary Magdalene was from the fishing village of Magdala and had been cured of seven evil spirits by Jesus (Luke 8:1–2). She was also one of the women set free from diseases and evil spirits who helped "to support [Jesus and His disciples] out of their own means" (v. 3 NIV; see also Mark 15:41). The other Mary is the mother of James and Joseph, which indicates that her sons were probably well known in the believing community. Salome was most likely the wife of Zebedee and mother of Jesus's disciples James and John (see Matthew 27:56). The gospel of John states that three Marys witnessed the crucifixion: Jesus's mother, His mother's sister (the wife of Clopas), and Mary Magdalene (19:25).

ENGAGE

As the women in today's passage were present to Jesus's life and death, where might you feel called to "stay near Jesus" in a life circumstance right now, whether in the face of temptation, suffering, or joy?

DAY 36

Mary Magdalene

JOHN 20:11–16, 18

Mary was standing outside the tomb crying, and as she wept, she stooped and looked in. She saw two white-robed angels, one sitting at the head and the other at the foot of the place where the body of Jesus had been lying. "Dear woman, why are you crying?" the angels asked her.

"Because they have taken away my Lord," she replied, "and I don't know where they have put him."

She turned to leave and saw someone standing there. It was Jesus, but she didn't recognize him. "Dear woman, why are you crying?" Jesus asked her. "Who are you looking for?"

She thought he was the gardener. "Sir," she said, "if you have taken him away, tell me where you have put him, and I will go and get him."

"Mary!" Jesus said.

She turned to him and cried out, "Rabboni!" (which is Hebrew for "Teacher"). . . .

Mary Magdalene found the disciples and told them, "I have seen the Lord!" Then she gave them his message.

GRIEF OVERTURNED

I have seen the Lord!

JOHN 20:18

According to Jim and Jamie Dutcher, filmmakers known for their knowledge of wolves, when happy, wolves wag their tails and romp about. But after the death of a pack member, they grieve for weeks. They visit the place where the pack member died, showing grief by their drooping tails and mournful howls.

Grief is a powerful emotion we've all experienced, particularly at the death of a loved one or of a treasured hope. Mary Magdalene experienced it. She'd traveled with and helped support Jesus and His disciples (Luke 8:1–3). But His cruel death on a cross separated them. The only thing left for Mary to do for Jesus was to finish anointing His body for burial—a task the Sabbath had interrupted. But imagine how Mary felt when she found not a lifeless, broken body but a living Savior! Though she hadn't at first recognized the man standing before her, when He spoke her name, she knew who He was—Jesus! Instantly, grief turned to joy. Mary now had joyful news to share: "I have seen the Lord!" (John 20:18).

Jesus entered our dark world to bring freedom and life. His resurrection celebrates that He accomplished what He set out to do. Like Mary, we too can celebrate His resurrection and share the good news: He's alive!

—Linda Washington

When have you experienced a time when your sadness turned to joy?

How can you celebrate God's great gifts of freedom and life today?

PROFILE: MARY MAGDALENE

Who was Mary Magdalene? Mary Magdalene's name simply suggests she was "Mary from the town of Magdala." Because she's only identified by where she was from, Mary Magdalene was likely a single woman when she joined Jesus's followers. Luke tells us Jesus cast seven demons from her (Luke 8:2).

A persistent myth about Mary Magdalene has been that she was a prostitute prior to following Jesus, a misconception dating back to Pope Gregory the Great, who in AD 591 preached that Mary Magdalene was the woman of poor reputation who anointed Jesus's feet (Luke 7:36–50). But there's no evidence Mary Magdalene was this woman.

Instead, Scripture consistently portrays Mary Magdalene only as a faithful disciple. She is identified at the foot of the cross (Matthew 27:56; Mark 15:40; John 19:25) and at Jesus's tomb (Matthew 27:61; 28:1–10; Mark 15:47–16:8; Luke 24:1–11; John 20:1–18).

Because she was given the tremendous honor of being the first in Scripture to encounter the risen Jesus and was entrusted with sharing the good news of Jesus's resurrection and coming ascension (John 20:18), Mary Magdalene is often called the "apostle to the apostles."

ENGAGE

In your imagination, enter into today's Bible story as Mary Magdalene. As you stand by the empty tomb, hear your name being called in an unmistakable voice as only He—your Savior—can say it. What is it like to hear your name spoken with such love? Feel your amazement and joy as you cry out, "Rabboni! Teacher!" How does He respond to your voice? What is His facial expression as He looks at you? What do you want to tell Him?

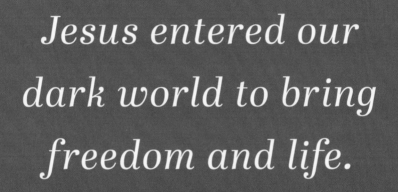

*Jesus entered our
dark world to bring
freedom and life.*

DAY 37

Tabitha

ACTS 9:36–42

There was a believer in Joppa named Tabitha (which in Greek is Dorcas). She was always doing kind things for others and helping the poor. About this time she became ill and died. Her body was washed for burial and laid in an upstairs room. But the believers had heard that Peter was nearby at Lydda, so they sent two men to beg him, "Please come as soon as possible!"

Disciple in many Bible translations; Greek *mathetria*; see today's word study.

So Peter returned with them; and as soon as he arrived, they took him to the upstairs room. The room was filled with widows who were weeping and showing him the coats and other clothes Dorcas had made for them. But Peter asked them all to leave the room; then he knelt and prayed. Turning to the body he said, "Get up, Tabitha." And she opened her eyes! When she saw Peter, she sat up! He gave her his hand and helped her up. Then he called in the widows and all the believers, and he presented her to them alive.

The news spread through the whole town, and many believed in the Lord.

A LEGACY OF KINDNESS

*There was a believer in Joppa named Tabitha
(which in Greek is Dorcas). She was always doing kind things
for others and helping the poor.*

ACTS 9:36

Martha served as a teacher's aide at an elementary school for over thirty years. Every year, she saved money to buy new coats, scarves, and gloves for students in need. After she lost her fight with leukemia, we held a celebration of life service. In lieu of flowers, people donated hundreds of brand-new winter coats to the students she loved and served for decades. Many people shared stories about the countless ways Martha encouraged others with kind words and thoughtful deeds. Her fellow teachers honored her memory with an annual coat drive for three years after her life ended on this side of eternity. Her legacy of kindness still inspires others to generously serve those in need.

In Acts 9, the apostle Luke shares a story about Tabitha, a woman who was "doing kind things for others and helping the poor" (v. 36). After she got sick and died, the grieving community urged Peter to visit. All the widows showed Peter how Tabitha had lived to serve (v. 39). In a miraculous act of compassion, God empowered Peter to bring Tabitha back to life. The news of Tabitha's resurrection spread, and "many believed in the Lord" (v. 42). But it was Tabitha's commitment to serving others in practical ways that touched the hearts in her community and revealed the power of loving generosity.

—Xochitl Dixon

How can you love someone with your kind words and deeds today?

_____

_____

_____

_____

_____

_____

How has God used someone else's kindness to draw you closer to Him?

_____

_____

_____

_____

_____

_____

_____

Word Study

DISCIPLE [NLT translation—*believer*]

mathetria (Acts 9:36)

Luke, the author of Acts, identifies Tabitha (or Dorcas in Greek) with the Greek word *mathetria*, which translates "believer" (NLT) or "disciple" (NIV). This word was used for someone under the training of a teacher. In the gospel of Luke, it's used to identify not just the twelve disciples but Jesus's other followers as well (14:25–27). In Acts, Luke uses it for believers in Jesus who are committed to living for and witnessing about the risen Savior, even at the risk of persecution (6:1–2; 9:1–2).

Tabitha is a beloved leader within the community of believers in the city of Joppa who devoted her life to acts of mercy and justice toward the economically vulnerable in her community, through work like providing clothing for widows (Acts 9:39). Tabitha's service, rooted in her faith, made her death a tremendous loss for her community (Acts 9:38–39). Her character and miraculous restoration to life (vv. 41–42) drew others to join the community of Jesus's disciples.

ENGAGE

As you reread Acts 9:36–42, pay attention to a word, phrase, or conversation that intrigues you. Ponder whatever particular phrase you choose, allowing God to speak to your heart and mind.

DAY 38

Lydia

ACTS 16:11–15

We boarded a boat at Troas and sailed straight across to the island of Samothrace, and the next day we landed at Neapolis. From there we reached Philippi, a major city of that district of Macedonia and a Roman colony. And we stayed there several days.

On the Sabbath we went a little way outside the city to a riverbank, where we thought people would be meeting for prayer, and we sat down to speak with some women who had gathered there. One of them was Lydia from Thyatira, a merchant of expensive purple cloth, who worshiped God. As she listened to us, the Lord opened her heart, and she accepted what Paul was saying. She and her household were baptized, and she asked us to be her guests. "If you agree that I am a true believer in the Lord," she said, "come and stay at my home." And she urged us until we agreed.

A SUCCESSFUL WOMAN

**The Lord opened her heart, and she accepted what
Paul was saying.**

ACTS 16:14

"It's an attractive offer, but I have to decline," I told my boss. Being made a business partner in the new subsidiary would definitely be a step up in my career. But knowing the long hours that entrepreneurs work, I was unwilling to take the plunge. I doubted I'd be able to do well at work and at home, without compromising my relationship with God.

Some people are able to do so, though. Lydia from the city of Thyatira was an example (Acts 16:11–15). She was a successful merchant in purple cloth with a big house that could accommodate the apostle Paul and his friends. When she trusted in Jesus, her household made the same commitment too. She was also a devout woman of prayer.

Whether we are as successful as Lydia or just struggling along, the good news is we can all be successful in the one thing that truly matters—a vibrant and living relationship with Jesus. In His grace, the Lord rerouted Paul from Asia and Bithynia to Macedonia (vv. 6–10). He then ensured that Lydia encountered Paul and heard the good news of Jesus. He "opened her heart" to receive the life-giving message (v. 14). Today, God is still divinely at work, drawing us near. Let's ask Him to open our hearts to respond to His Word that we may find new strength from knowing all that Christ has done and is doing for us.

—Poh Fang Chia

How is God calling you to steward your gifts, as Lydia did? Tell God you're committed to stewarding them well.

_____

_____

_____

_____

_____

_____

What is God's definition of success for you? Talk to Him about it.

_____

_____

_____

_____

_____

_____

_____

WOMEN IN BUSINESS

Although in Greco-Roman households husbands had the highest degree of authority and power, Roman law gave free women many rights to not only manage their households but participate in society, including in business. In cities, both men and women could be found working in various trades.

Macedonia, the area of Greece where Paul met Lydia, was well known for having women of wealth and social and religious influence.

Lydia was likely one such woman. She is a dealer of purple cloth, a luxury product that Thyatira, the city in Asia Minor that Lydia was from (Acts 16:14), was well known for. We're also told she "worshiped God" (v. 14), likely meaning that, like Cornelius (10:1–2), she was a gentile sympathetic to Judaism.

Lydia is described as having her own household (16:15), which suggests she was likely a prosperous freedwoman, widow, or divorcée. Lydia's home appears to have become a house church after her conversion (v. 40). Another woman in Scripture who may have been a profitable businesswoman is Phoebe, a woman of means who supported many believers (Romans 16:1–2).

ENGAGE

The devotional author discusses different definitions of success. List a few things that you have believed would make you successful.

- _____
- _____
- _____
- _____
- _____
- _____
- _____
- _____
- _____
- _____

God, please give me Your definition of success for me. Help me to know that I'm accepted and loved no matter what. I ask that I can live freely out of Your incredible grace and unfailing love. In Jesus's name, amen.

We can all be successful in the one thing that truly matters—a vibrant and living relationship with Jesus.

DAY 39

Phoebe

ROMANS 16:1–2

I commend to you our sister Phoebe, who is a deacon in the church in Cenchrea. Welcome her in the Lord as one who is worthy of honor among God's people. Help her in whatever she needs, for she has been **helpful** to many, and especially to me.

Greek *prostratis*; see today's biblical insight: The Distribution of an Epistle.

FAITHFUL PHOEBE

I commend to you our sister Phoebe.

ROMANS 16:1

Applying for jobs right out of college was challenging because I needed to introduce myself to potential employers who didn't know me. With a limited resume of internships and class projects, I took the advice of an advisor and requested a letter of recommendation from the university president. His gracious letter outlining my faithfulness on a project I had worked on for him greatly encouraged me in my job search.

When the apostle Paul closed his letter to the Romans, he wrote several personal greetings to the people who would read his letter. But first, he started with a recommendation of the woman who, according to church tradition, took on the important job to deliver the letter.

We don't know much about Phoebe, but we have a glimpse of her character and work in Paul's powerful recommendation. Paul wrote that she was "a deacon in the church" (Romans 16:1) in Greece, demonstrating her willingness to serve. He affirmed that Phoebe was worthy of the Roman church's assistance (v. 2) and commended her generous giving, noting that she was "the benefactor of many people, including me" (v. 2 NIV). Because Phoebe served faithfully in Greece, Paul confidently commended her to the Roman church, a recommendation that allowed her to be warmly welcomed as a sister in Christ.

Phoebe's legacy encourages us that not only does serving allow us to experience joy, but it opens doors for us to be a blessing to others.

—Lisa M. Samra

ENGAGE

Identify someone in your life who, like Phoebe, has been a great support and encouragement to you. Take time to journal, thanking God for them and for their life-changing role.

_____

_____

_____

_____

_____

In what ways has your service opened doors to bless others?

_____

_____

_____

_____

_____

_____

_____

_____

THE DISTRIBUTION OF AN EPISTLE

The Roman empire had a mail system, but its use was normally limited to government mail. That meant that nearly all letters required someone to personally travel to deliver the letter. Sometimes letters were written specifically because someone was already traveling that way.

Paul could have chosen Phoebe to deliver the letter to the Romans for many reasons, including her work as a deacon (Romans 16:1) and her history of generosity and hospitality (v. 2). The word translated "helpful" in verse 2 by the NLT is the Greek *prostratis*, which can also be translated "patron" (ESV). In the Greco-Roman world of Paul's day, patrons—people with the means to support others in the arts and other endeavors—were widely relied on and honored for their generosity. Phoebe appears to have been someone with the resources to support "many," including Paul (v. 2). She might have been a profitable businesswoman who would travel for her work between Corinth and Rome, which had close trade ties.

Phoebe may also have been chosen due to a gift for public speaking. At that time, the person delivering a letter to a group would normally also present its contents, since many in the group likely could not read. The letter reader could also serve as an interpreter, given authority by the author to clarify any questions about the letter. Phoebe would likely have spent significant time practicing her delivery of this incredibly important letter before beginning her journey.

Phoebe could have delivered Paul's letter by traveling on foot (an approximately six- to eight-week journey) or, more likely, by traveling by ship from Corinth to Rome in under two weeks.

DAY 40

Priscilla

ACTS 18:1–3, 18–19, 24–26; ROMANS 16:3–5

Then Paul left Athens and went to Corinth. There he became acquainted with a Jew named Aquila, born in Pontus, who had recently arrived from Italy with his wife, Priscilla. They had left Italy when Claudius Caesar deported all Jews from Rome. Paul lived and worked with them, for they were tentmakers just as he was. . . . Then [Paul] set sail for Syria, taking Priscilla and Aquila with him.

They stopped first at the port of Ephesus, where Paul left the others behind. . . .

Meanwhile, a Jew named Apollos, an eloquent speaker who knew the Scriptures well, had arrived in Ephesus from Alexandria in Egypt. He had been taught the way of the Lord, and he taught others about Jesus with an enthusiastic spirit and with accuracy. However, he knew only about John's baptism. When Priscilla and Aquila heard him preaching boldly in the synagogue, they took him aside and explained the way of God even more accurately.

Give my greetings to Priscilla and Aquila, my co-workers in the ministry of Christ Jesus. In fact, they once | Greek *synergos*; see today's word study.

risked their lives for me. I am thankful to them, and so are all the Gentile churches. Also give my greetings to the church that meets in their home.

CO-WORKERS FOR GOD

When Priscilla and Aquila heard him preaching boldly in the synagogue, they took him aside and explained the way of God even more accurately.

ACTS 18:26

William and Catherine Booth worked together to spark a movement of reform in nineteenth-century England, which became the Salvation Army. Motivated by their faith in God, they sought to better the life of the poor and downtrodden, whether through William providing meals to the hungry or Catherine seeking to fund their activities via financial help from wealthy women. When speaking of their pioneering work today, we most often name them as a pair.

Another couple who are always mentioned together in the New Testament are Priscilla and Aquila—with Priscilla named first four of six times, which probably indicates her powerful influence. The apostle Paul met them in Corinth after they had to leave their home network of Rome when Claudius exiled all Jewish people (Acts 18:2). Paul called them his "co-workers in the ministry of Christ Jesus" (Romans 16:3); they were fellow tentmakers and missionaries who joined him on one of his missionary journeys and who continued their work in Ephesus (Acts 18:18–19). They risked their lives for him (Romans 16:4), gently mentored a fiery preacher who hadn't heard the full story of Jesus (Acts 18:26), and hosted a home church for many years.

Both couples were ordinary people doing extraordinary things for God, with His help. Whether we're serving God as part of a married couple or on our own, we can trust that He will empower us to make a difference for Him.

—Amy Boucher Pye

At the beginning of your forty-day journey, we reflected on the questions God asked Hagar: "Where have you come from, and where are you going?" As this devotional study comes to a close, focus especially on the second question—"Where are you going?"

With God, look at the anticipated highlights in the days ahead: What is the scenery in front of you, the landscapes, the potential delays (and how about the weather)? As you share with God your hopes, dreams, and fears about your upcoming journey, be reminded that He cares for every detail of your life, He is fiercely protective of you, and He is making a way for you.

Word Study

CO-WORKERS

synergos (Romans 16:3)

Paul refers to Priscilla and Aquila as ministry "co-workers" (Romans 16:3), which is the plural form of the Greek word *synergos*. Sometimes translated "worker," "co-worker," or "fellow worker," it's a word used almost exclusively by Paul in the New Testament (see, for example, 1 Thessalonians 3:2; Romans 16:9, 21; Philippians 2:25; and Philemon 24). Paul uses this word not to describe believers in Jesus in general, but to identify church leaders with authority. In 1 Corinthians 3:9, for example, Paul describes leaders like him and Apollos as God's "workers" (plural of *synergos*), while other believers who benefit from their leadership are "God's field." In 1 Corinthians 16:16, similarly, Paul urges believers to submit to the leadership of every "fellow worker" (ESV).

Both Priscilla and Aquila were among those whom Paul counted as trusted ministry leaders, whose work was essential for spreading and establishing the gospel among the gentiles (Romans 16:4).

ENGAGE

*Loving God, You have given me passions and gifts that
I want to use for Your glory. Help me to serve You
with joy and perseverance.*

Tell God what you need to keep pressing in.

_____

_____

_____

_____

_____

_____

_____

_____

_____

_____

_____

_____

*Thank You for providing for everything I need.
In Jesus's name, amen.*

God cares for every detail of your life, He is fiercely protective of you, and He is making a way for you.

known
by
God

Contributors

To learn more about the writers of *Our Daily Bread*,
visit odb.org/all-authors.

Julie Ackerman Link

Jennifer Benson Schuldt

Amy Boucher Pye

Anne Cetas

Xochitl Dixon

Poh Fang Chia

Cindy Hess Kasper

Kirsten Holmberg

Alyson Kieda

Monica La Rose

Elisa Morgan

Katara Patton

Patricia Raybon

Lisa M. Samra

Marion Stroud

Linda Washington

Anna Haggard, General Editor, is associate content editor for Our Daily Bread Publishing. A follower of Jesus, she loves to write and edit books sharing about God's generous, deep love for all people. Anna coauthored the Called and Courageous Girls series, and she lives in Grand Rapids, Michigan.

Monica La Rose, Theological Content Editor, is a writer and editor for Our Daily Bread Ministries. A graduate of Calvin Theological Seminary, Monica has a Master of Theological Studies degree and is a devotional writer for *Our Daily Bread*. She and her husband live in the Chicago area.

Patti Brinks, Designer, is art director for Our Daily Bread Ministries. A graduate of Kendall College of Art and Design, she has collaborated with numerous *New York Times* best-selling authors during her years in publishing. Patti and her husband live in the Grand Rapids area and have two wonderful daughters and sons-in-law and one grandson.

Help us get the word out!

Our Daily Bread Publishing exists to feed the soul with the Word of God.

If you appreciated this book, please let others know.

- Pick up another copy to give as a gift.
- Share a link to the book or mention it on social media.
- Write a review on your blog, on a book-seller's website, or at our own site (odb.org/store).
- Recommend this book for your church, book club, or small group.

Connect with us:

- @ourdailybread
- @ourdailybread
- @ourdailybread

Our Daily Bread Publishing
PO Box 3566
Grand Rapids, Michigan 49501 USA

- books@odb.org